Merry Christmas 199 to

Charlie from Brother-in-law Jim

— Wishing you Good Hunting
in the New Year!

WESTERN
Skies

WESTERN *Skies*

JOHN BARSNESS

Lyons & Burford, Publishers

FOR MY MOTHER

who cooked the jackrabbit

Much of this book appeared, in different form, in *Field & Stream*, *Game Journal*,
Gray's Sporting Journal, *Shooting Sportsman*, *Sports Afield*, *Wing & Shot* and *Wyoming
Wildlife*.

Design by Cindy LaBreacht
Printed in the United States of America
10 9 8 7 6 5 4 3 2 1

Library of Congress Cataloging-in-Publication Data

Barsness, John.
Western skies / John Barsness.
p. cm.
ISBN 1-55821-307-4
1. Fowling—West (U.S.) 2. Natural History—West (U.S.)
I. Title.
SK313.B37 1994
799.2'4'0978—dc20   94-11159
CIP

CONTENTS

INTRODUCTION

Wild Game

"In all revolutions, the first thing the 'people' have done was to jump over the fences of the preserves or to tear them down, and in the name of social justice pursue the hare and partridge."

—JOSÉ ORTEGA Y GASSET
Meditations on Hunting

There's a remote canyon in southern Arizona that ends as a dry wash down in a river valley. A two-track road runs along the south side of the wash, passing through a saguaro forest on its way toward the brown mountains beyond, the cactus as tall and thick as big oaks, though the bare arms offer no shade. Above the saguaros the ridges are covered with barrel cactus and paloverde and then, as the road reaches toward the mountains, the wash deepens into a miniature version of the canyon we call Grand, except without the tourists and California smog. It does have desert bighorn sheep, coyotes, javelinas, roadrunners, mule deer, and the small whitetail we call Coues. Oh, and two kinds of quail, the excuse for being there.

It is quite a fine place to camp and hunt, particularly in the spring green of February after already enduring part of a winter in the northern Rockies. You start in the early morning wearing a flannel-lined denim jacket, then stuff it in your game bag as the temperature rises. At noon you sit under the shade of the small oaks around a waterhole, listening to the quail you scattered from near the water, their brothers and sisters in the game bag next to your jacket, the dog standing in a coyote's tracks as he drinks from the waterhole. At night you cook quail over a mesquite fire and look at as much galaxy as you're likely to see in this particular part of the twentieth century.

After several days of this pleasant life, you drive slowly back down the two-track to the gravel road and, at the breakneck speed of forty miles per hour, head toward Tucson and a shower. Fifteen miles later you come around a bend to see the billboard of a pheasant preserve. You missed this on the way in, perhaps because it's backed into the cottonwoods at an odd angle, perhaps you didn't want to. Braking the pickup in hot dust, you read the sign's fine print: there's also a Sporting Clays layout to sharpen city shooters before they kill their paid allotment of pen-raised birds. After three days of hunting and eating wild quail on public land, you puzzle at this, and for quite a long while.

Why would anyone prefer to shoot tame pheasants in a place pheasants cannot naturally exist, when all around are thousands of acres of public land holding wild quail? Part of the answer, I suspect, lies in the ringnecked pheasant, which for decades has been the ideal of the American bird hunter. Since the ringneck isn't native to America, this may seem odd—until you reflect that no humans are, either, "Native Americans" included.

But most of the answer lies in us, the American hunter. Despite those who regard us as anachronisms, we are as much a part of modern America as anyone who watches TV and buys *People* magazine. Despite democratic ideals, like the rest of humanity America has always been a society divided by money, if not as vastly as much of the "undeveloped" world, where there is no middle class, just the very poor and the very rich. The difference between America and most of the world is that our society was designed around the possibility of upward mobility, where being poor or rich depends on our abilities and not whether our parents are peasants or kings.

As Ortega y Gasset points out, it is the nature of the monied leisure class to hunt. "This what kings and nobles have preferred to do: they have hunted." Traditionally, such folks have hunted on their own preserves, or outlawed certain animals to the peasantry, one of the reasons Robin Hood was an outlaw. He poached the King's deer, and other "noble" game. This reserving of the best hunting for those in power has continued through the centuries. The Shah of Iran had his own preserves, where he entertained heads of state, actors, hunting writers, and other dictators and despots. The Queen of England has her own hunting lands and dogs. When

George Bush hunts, he doesn't do it on state lands, but exclusive ranches in Texas. Those of us not quite so blessed with power and wealth have always made do with what's left over, whether poaching hares in Ireland or hunting sage grouse on the public deserts of Wyoming.

Of course, at least some of the roots of our country lie in the tradition of a "right" to hunt, born out of both a resentment of European monarchies and our own bountiful wild land and game. But as our population grows, more and more people hunt the "commons," the state and national forests, the wildlife refuges, the Bureau of Land Management deserts.

As we crowd more and more onto public hunting lands, that nebulous something one of my friends calls The Quality Outdoor Experience grows more rare. As more people use less, more laws are passed, some to preserve that quality, and some to preserve anything at all, stifling the freedom that is an intrinsic part of The Quality Outdoor. This crowding and regulation doesn't only apply to hunting. These days we have to apply a year ahead for reservations to camp in Yosemite National Park, and something similar is going to happen to Yellowstone very soon. As public forests in the East grow not just crowded but actually dangerous to hunt in, more and more hunters come West, to hunt forests already crowded by folks who moved to Wyoming and Idaho and Montana to get away from a crowded California.

And so it goes. Those of us who were lucky enough to be raised somewhere close to the land, with a sense of self-

WILD GAME / 11

sufficiency and (dare I say it?) The Quality Outdoor Experience, just go deeper. That can mean hiking farther into the Wind River Range, moving to Alaska, or just hunting something not so damn popular, like sage grouse.

But most of America wasn't raised on a farm or anywhere near a forest. Most of America was raised within asphalt distance of a movie theater or, these days, a video store. Most of America gets it values from *Lifestyles Of The Rich and Famous*. Most of America "recreates" in cities, where fun usually involves paying money to be entertained while sitting down.

The suburbanite's desire to hunt must be deeply instinctive if it isn't buried by a world according to Trump. But the corollary must be that when modern America decides to hunt, it wants a sure thing. A place where your dollar always buys satisfaction, where if you pay for three pheasants you by God kill three pheasants.

So after puzzling for a while on why anyone would want to pay to hunt tame pheasants when there is much better "free" hunting for wild quail all around them, I've quit being puzzled. The modern urban American hunter wants something certain, and in modern America a few dollars searching for something certain will find it. That's the law of the marketplace, and the marketplace has created Natty Bumppo as comparison shopper.

But anyone who has hiked miles of dry Wyoming after sage hens, or pushed through hillsides of briars after ruffed grouse, or chased wild pheasants out of cattail swamps, knows that a credit-card pheasant has as much to with hunting as watching a video. No matter how uneducated, a hunter who pays for hunting in boot leather gains a gut-level understanding of wild lives; if education and travel allow, that same hunter may come to assimilate the collection of molecules and sunlight we call the biosphere as deeply as anyone alive. It is precisely the difference between two of our presidents, that essential hunter-naturalist Theodore Roosevelt and our recent "environmental president," George Bush. To dance with any grace, you must learn the steps, not pay the musician.

The hunter-naturalist's life chose me long ago, beginning with a child's instincts and ending perilously close to both science and religion, influenced not so much by Natty Bumppo as by Meriwether Lewis and William Clark, Theodore Roosevelt, Black Elk, Aldo Leopold, Roger Tory Peterson, and Wendell Berry. Hunting wild birds sustains my life, as does growing my garden, writing stories, driving obscure western highways, and the woman who hunts with me. Each brings more joy than any marketplace. These stories are not apologies for that life, but celebrations, because that is what hunting wild birds should be.

—John Barsness
Townsend, Montana

1

Where the Sky Began

HOMESTEADER'S JACKRABBIT STEW:
Get yourself a good big winter jackrabbit and
a five-pound rock. Skin the rabbit and wash
the rock, then put them both in a big pot.
Boil 'em until you can stick a fork in the rock,
then throw away the rabbit and eat the rock.

Now it is grazing land, high pastures of blue grama grass and
sagebrush suspended between mountain ranges that rise like
snowy lighthouses in the distance, but back around the turn
of the century people thought they could grow wheat there.
My grandmother was one: she came from Minnesota in 1912
and put in a half-section claim near Roy, Montana, a little
town on the north side of the Judith Range. Roy isn't very big
now—there isn't even a population listed for it on the official
state highway map—and it wasn't much bigger then, but that
didn't matter much because she lived by herself out on the
homestead. After a while, a Norwegian homesteaded nearby,

and after another while she married him and they had two sons.

My father came along second, just in time to grow up during the Depression, and one of his memories of that bleak time was of bouncing across the plains in a Model A Ford filled with men, guns, and my grandmother. He remembered getting out of the car last—he was only eight, wedged tightly between big men dressed in wool coats that were still flecked with wheat straw—on a cold day, the wind whipping the sage, the booming of shotguns and the sage hens still flying until Grandma's little Winchester twenty-two pump went "ptt ptt ptt" and three huge sage grouse fell out of the air. Shotshells were expensive then and I imagine the men didn't practice much, but Grandma had a reputation with any kind of rifle and used one long after shotshells grew easier to come by. During the worst times, the family ate jackrabbits instead of sage hens: because even during the constant shortages of the Depression, there was never a shortage of whitetailed jacks. I killed my first edible game at the age of twelve, a young jackrabbit taken just outside the city limits with my own twenty-two. I gutted and skinned it, and then my mother cooked it up in a stew. All through supper my father asked what sort of good meat this was, but my mother delayed telling him until the end of the meal. He went straight into the bathroom and tossed it up.

My father's next bird-hunting memory came from a half-dozen years later, after Grandpa had died. I'd like to think the memory came from a lack of fatherly guidance, but more likely it was just joy-shooting by fool kids. Four of them, my father and three friends, were riding in another Model A along a country road after just having ground-sluiced a road sign or some other inedible object. My dad was in the backseat, trying to reload Grandpa's old Stevens double gun, when the Model A bounced out of a particularly deep pothole and the shotgun slammed shut. The locking lever sliced over the web of his thumb, and he instinctively jerked his fingers, which happened to be over the triggers. The shotgun went boom—or rather BOOM because both barrels went off at once—and a four-inch hole appeared in the bottom of the car. They had a hard time explaining *that*, along with all the blood over the backseat, especially since they didn't come home with any game, not even a jackrabbit.

The old double hung for years on the wall above the kitchen door, until I inexplicably got the urge to shoot birds with it. My father hadn't turned out to be much of a bird hunter, maybe because of the experience inside the Model A, but perhaps more because of a homesteader's son's conviction that it wasn't worth the time and effort to shoot one-pound birds with expensive shotshells. Despite a Ph.D. and university-department-head's salary, he always thought it more pragmatic to hunt deer if you wanted wild meat, even though with a rifle he still managed to shoot holes in the wrong places. He was checking out his thirty-thirty one fall day before the season opened and slammed the action shut with his finger on the trigger, the bullet burying itself in the brick wall of our old Victorian house. Was it leftover damn foolishness from youth, or the absentmindedness of a college professor? I never grew big enough to ask; like his father, he died young. His mother never did shoot holes in anything she didn't want to.

What makes so many of us reject the world our parents carefully carved and skip back a generation or three? For some reason I found more of value in sage grouse and shotguns than university halls, more aesthetics in the smell of sagebrush than a discussion of American literature, though I did not reject the literature itself. By the time I should have been hell-bent for graduate school, I was back on the high plains with a Labrador retriever and Grandpa's old double gun. Unregenerate, my father would have snorted, but I think in some ways he would have envied me, too.

I guess dogs were the first specter of civilization out there in the grama grass. Bird dogs are the first sign that anyone is going hunting for something more than just a meal. Dogs turn the unpredictable chance at a flock of sage or sharptailed grouse into a more ritualized dance, bridging the gap between bird and man.

There were bird dogs back then, but not too many, because it was a tough time and place to be making a living, and the trappings of a sporting life were considered by most folks as unaffordable and probably sinful luxuries. And some of the wastrels that actually owned "real" bird dogs back then were in the cut-and-try stages of both dog training and understanding of Western birds. One old-timer I hunted with by the North Dakota border advised me to never, ever get hold of one of those Chesapeake dogs, because he'd had one back in the thirties that was so stubborn and ornery that it finally refused to get out of the back of the pickup one day during a sharptail expedition. My friend finally tried to lasso the dog and drag it out by main force—he'd grown up on a ranch—and almost got his hand bitten off for his trouble. It's an image that attacks me on the verge of sleep some nights: a leather-faced cowboy whirling a rope around his head on an empty prairie ridge, preparing to toss the loop at the head of a bull-necked Chesapeake Bay retriever braced sullenly in the back of an ancient Chevrolet pickup—probably at about the same time another hunter, a couple thousand miles to the southeast, ate a leisurely sandwich from the lunch box of a mule-drawn wagon, while his well-trained pointin' dogs searched for yet another covey of quail.

Some folks out here are still cutting and trying. Another friend, a farm-raised fellow from the Yellowstone River country in eastern Montana, more recently ventured down to Oklahoma to hunt quail with some in-laws. He was so impressed with some of the pointers he hunted over that he brought a Viszla back to Montana. On opening day of sharp-tail season, six of us were strung out across a hundred-acre stubblefield, with the dogs—two Labs and the Viszla— working out ahead. A third of the way across the field, the

Viszla suddenly went on point, then broke wildly and bit the porcupine he'd pointed right on the back. The sharptails went up two hundred yards away, frightened out of their wits at that poor dog's howls. I later heard that the Viszla became a fair pheasant dog, but never did learn to leave porcupines alone.

Of course, part of the problem, way back when, of working out a good dog solution to western hunting was that about the time people began using more practical dogs than Chesapeakes, new birds began showing up. The first was the ring-necked pheasant, released in Oregon in 1881, but not really well distributed over the rest of the West until somewhat later. Evidence that pheasant-planting and basic theory of game management were still in their infancy on the high plains came from my old Chesapeake-cursing friend during a cold November sharptail hunt, when he told me of the first pheasant releases in his part of the country. It was a big event, evidently, because not only did the whole county (perhaps three thousand people, all of whom owned a fowling piece of some sort) know of the impending arrival of a boxcar full of pheasants, but they also knew that the train was to stop three miles out of town on a rail spur, where the birds would be released. Several dozen sporting gentlemen were on hand with twelve-gauge pumps and high-brass fours to drop the birds as they rocketed out of the boxcar door. As near as my old friend could remember, he got eight or nine birds that day. The date was around 1925.

In spite of that incident and others of the same sort (I still see occasional notices in small Western newspapers that a batch of pheasants will be planted around Deep Coulee or Box Elder Crick on the first of the month, and *please* leave them alone until they can raise a few youngsters), pheasants got a toehold in the creekbottoms, wheatfields, and buffalo-berry thickets of much of the West, which was a good thing in most hunters' eyes because utilitarian shooting (poaching and market hunting) and habitat changes (erosion caused by over-plowing and -grazing) reduced the population of native birds. Many hunters hadn't thought too much of sage hens, sharptails, and prairie chickens anyway, and a white-meated bird that could live next door to a ranch house seemed nicely civilized, especially to the Depression-era ranch wives who had to cook whatever their husbands shot. A pheasant on the table must have reminded them of places where people always used the nice china and the land was tamed by cities and truck farms, rather than just recently wrested from Indians and buffalo and covered rather loosely by sagebrush.

After the great pheasant invasion came waves of Hungarian and chukar partridge. Most of the Huns or gray partridge on the high plains probably came from some 1908 and 1909 Alberta plantings. They found the American steppe so similar to their Eastern Europe homeland that by the 1920s they'd established themselves across the whole northern tier of the United States and the southern prairie provinces. In 1935 someone let a few chukar go in Nevada, and the birds soon spread to wherever the land was dry and tilted, just as it was in their native Central Asia.

Neither kind of partridge has ever overtaken the popularity of the pheasant, though, probably because—in the case of the chukar—the country's too tough and both birds are rather small. I encountered the first covey of Huns in my life at age sixteen on the shoulder of a gravel road near the Tongue River. My older (age twenty) hunting partner, a native of the region, jumped out of the pickup and ground-sluiced the bunch as they sat huddled by the roadside weeds, something he'd never do to a pheasant or even a sharptail. "Ain't enough meat on them 'little chickens' to waste shells shootin' 'em in the air," he said. A practical view, if nothing else: with one measly shell he "harvested" all his limit and half of mine.

Is it really any wonder that people still argue about the best Western bird dog, when "bird" means anything from a circle of Huns crouched like bobwhites in a rose coulee on the flat Dakota plain, a covey of chukar on a basalt knob a thousand feet straight up from the Salmon River in Idaho, to a flock of a hundred sage grouse migrating from the margins of mile-foot valleys in western Montana to pastures covered by miles and miles of sage? Some folks I know have tried using different dogs for different game—a German shorthair, for instance, might be just the item for Huns in the wheat country of western North Dakota, where you can find a covey in the same place year after year and the birds act as civilized as their European breeding. But pheasants in cottonwood creekbottoms or sharptails in badlands buffalo-berry thickets are an entirely different sort of ornithological pursuit, not to mention chukars on cliffs. One friend ran both a Lab and a Brittany for a while and spent more time shuffling dogs than hunting birds because sometimes he'd hunt three or four species in the same day. Most strictly upland hunters I know use a pointer like a Brittany spaniel or German shorthair, but those of us who hunt everything, from Huns to geese, generally use a Lab or golden retriever. These retrievers and their masters fit rather loosely into the general western landscape, proving the ecological theory that generalists—not specialists—tend to thrive under varied and changing conditions.

My canine partner for the first decade of my bird-chasing career was a lean and energetic black Labrador named Gillis, who was raised on sharptailed grouse, pheasants, and Huns on the plains of eastern Montana, with occasional side forays involving jump-shooting mallards, hot sage grouse walks, and chukars in Wyoming. He seemed equally happy flushing sharptails from buffalo-berries, playing ring-around-the-rosy with a rooster pheasant in a creekbottom rose thicket, or nudging Huns out of wheat stubble. Only once did he seem out of his element, when at the age of seven he first hunted ducks over decoys. A mallard fell and Gillis jumped in and grabbed a Styrofoam decoy. He was embarrassed and refused to ever retrieve decoys again, even when I wanted him to go out for one in water over my chest waders.

He hunted until he was almost fourteen, though very slowly and deafly in his last year, and for a while I considered some sort of pointing dog as replacement. But then all the birds called again, the doves and the Huns and the grouse and geese, and my new dog is a large chocolate Lab named Keith who has already retrieved most of the same birds.

Can there be a sporting tradition as strong in the West as it is for quail in the South or pa'tridge in New England, given such a variety of country and birds? In a land wrested so recently from hunting nomads and in some places still in the hands of pragmatic flock-shooting ranchers? A friend of mine, who grew up in a logging town near the Idaho border, recently sold a motorcycle to buy an expensive European side-by-side twelve-gauge, a step up from the standard full-choke, pump-action "meat gun" that's long graced pickup windows across the West, but I'll bet you a bottle of good bourbon that he'll be tempted to ground-sluice a covey of Huns if he gets the chance. Even this unregenerate home-steader's grandson now carries a fancy sidelock double gun, with which I miss much more often than my grandmother ever did with her twenty-two rifle.

If tradition grows from moments that form the most pleasant and valued memories, yes, there can be a Western bird-hunting tradition. But it must begin with the acceptance of the difference between East and West, which the historian Wallace Stegner defined as "aridity." The average bird-hunter, or indeed anyone who grew up to the right of the

100th meridian, the arbitrary boundary of the West that roughly divides the Dakotas in half, cannot ever really comprehend our Great American Desert until they spend some years here. (Even then it sometimes does not get through. The early history of agriculture in the West, inevitably tied to the welfare of upland gamebirds, is one of stubborn refusal to accept the fact that high plains rain is a sporadic and temporary phenomenon. This refusal ended in the Dust Bowl, just as the flocks of thousands of prairie chickens ended under the plow.)

My most ingrained memory is arid indeed—even in bird-chasers' terms, since not a single shot was fired—the end of a long day after sharptails in the breaks above one of the Missouri tributaries. The sun was going down behind a pyramid butte to the west, men and dogs on a sagebrush ridge above a long coulee where a spring fed two small cottonwoods. One of us spotted several grouse in the short sage of a hillside two hundred yards away, and then another covey came floating down one of the side coulees toward the water, dull feathers turned almost red by the last sun, then suddenly turning dark as they glided into the blue shadow of the draw. We walked to the highest ridge, and the first bunch flushed ragged and wild and then coasted downhill toward the spring; and then yet another wild bunch rose, a ridge away. First six birds, then three, then scattered singles, and then from all around us, across the miles of coulees that centered on the green spring, wild grouse rose and sailed along the ridges and down the draws toward the water, as if they were streams in themselves, flowing downward to the sea. Somewhere beyond the ridges and draws there may have been a fenceline, or perhaps an old homestead, but only somewhere beyond the sunset, beyond where men and dogs could see.

2

The Grouse Nobody Knows

The prairie appears to be ocean from up there, where the highway leaves the pine hills that divide the Yellowstone and Musselshell rivers, especially after the winter solstice when the days move toward variations of gray. The sky on that particular day could have come from the coast of Oregon or Maine, with clouds so flat and low that sunlight from above turned them into a pearl neon. The hills below the sky rose in parallel waves as barren as iron, tilted sediments from a real Mesozoic seabottom, grass removed by summer cattle and most snow removed by wind, except for a few particles of black caught between the sea and sky where the light was brightest, toward the west.

They were big birds and at first I though they were mallards. But they didn't fly with the greenhead's steady autopilot, twisting in the wind more like giant teal. Though their silhouettes were precise under the neon clouds, it wasn't until they flew within a hundred yards that I realized they were sage grouse. They flew almost over the vehicle, never reacting, and kept flying until they merged into the distant gray like a flock of noonday falling stars.

That's the way most hunters meet sage grouse—one swift passing on the high plains—the reason we do not know them at all well. Even those who enter the sage ocean to hunt big grouse often do so only for a day or two, to say they did it. I've read many accounts by pilgrims who follow a local rancher (who doesn't hunt the "sage chickens" himself, but knows where they hang out) to a flock of birds of the year on a dusty September afternoon, the birds asleep under the tall sage below a stock dam. The hunter "harvests" one or two on the first slow flush, then declines to chase the covey farther because (he implies) this would destroy a rare national treasure. Actually, he just wants to chase ruffed grouse in the far mountains he can see dancing so tantalizingly in heat mirage, or pheasants along the riverbottom grainfields, or some other Real Gamebird in some place other than a hot, endless sagebrush desert. The feeling is that sage grouse make an interesting novelty item—something like collecting a couple of conchs on a Bahamian vacation—but they are not a bird to get all fussed up about.

A few Novembers ago a friend of a friend, a surgeon from the West Coast who had hunted birds across the country but never collected such a novelty, came through central Montana. Over the phone we arranged to meet at a truck stop in a small ranching community. He was worried that we'd never find each other, but I reassured him he couldn't miss it, since there wasn't much else out there. Urban visitors often react that way where there are no street signs, or any landmarks except sagebrush, as far as the next horizon, twenty miles away.

We met early in the morning and took a gravel road through sage-grouse country. At the first big coulee I pulled my pickup over. There was a big stock dam a half-mile up the coulee, and the "crick" almost always held some sage grouse, either below or above the reservoir. I leaned against the doctor's car while he loaded his well-used pump—he gave a short commentary on how many birds it had taken, from Mexico to Canada—and then unloaded my old black Lab from the truck. We'd walked perhaps a hundred yards up the coulee when Gillis's tail began acting like a drunken metronome, and then half the sagebrush along the dry creek rose and spread its wings. The good doctor half-raised his shotgun, never having seen a hundred grouse the size of young turkeys flush from almost-barren ground, and missed. Then he lowered the shotgun, saying something I couldn't hear to his trusty pumpgun as three or four dozen more sage grouse sailed toward the next un-road-signed horizon.

I confess I laughed a little. After the last bird disappeared, he turned toward me, saying, "Shotgun jammed. It's never done that before." I didn't say anything. He hesitated, then said, "I guess I got a little excited."

I shrugged. "If we don't get excited, what's the point?"

One point is that any of us—pilgrim, surgeon, or native of the high plains—would gather different views of sage grouse from our individual meetings. They could be large, slow, easy-to-shoot relics of a wilderness past (something like buffalo with wings), or run in vast disquieting herds (something like Cape buffalo with wings), or be the only grouse that migrates. The truth is they can be all three, and more.

But even if we encounter all those variations in a grouse, we never really know them. We can kill a big male sage grouse and feel his improbable weight (there is no better definition of specific density than a brace of mature sage roosters, three or four hot miles from a pickup) and smell his acrid blood, like railroad ties on a hot day, but the birds will always remain strangers. No, let me correct that. We will always remain strangers in their land. We've never really accepted their sagebrush ocean—"wastes," we often called them, in our journals of exploration—and so never really accepted the birds, since they are the essence of sage.

Humanity's relationship with sagebrush is reminiscent of the conflicts of surface geology: the pressures from inside the earth building mountains and valleys, while wind and rain and oceans try to smooth everything out. We've always hated sage, poisoning and ripping and burning it, meanwhile overgrazing grasslands until sagebrush invades the abused vacuum. Lately we have come belatedly to find that natural sage flats produce more grass (and hence beef, lamb, and wool, not to mention pronghorns and sage grouse) than chained or poisoned flats. The sagebrush retains winter snow that otherwise would blow into the nearest coulee and run off into the Missouri come spring. Just as hunters are always relearning to trust their bird dog's noses, humanity keeps relearning to trust the tendencies of nature.

Since sage grouse are tied inexorably to sage—it forms almost their entire diet during winter—our attempts to kill the natural sagelands almost killed off the birds. But after we dumped a zillion cattle on the freshly bisonless plains, sage made a comeback, often where it never thrived before. So did the grouse, especially after every homesteader quit salting down a barrel or two each November. As anybody who's driven across Wyoming and Nevada knows, we don't lack for sagebrush. Hence we don't lack for sage birds, even in some unlikely places, such as the high deserts along the eastern border of California. It helps to remember that they are *desert* birds, and like desert forbs they can disappear almost completely during drought, only to replicate madly with a little rain. I have hunted the same piece of BLM sage for half-a-dozen autumns now. In most years you can find a covey or two in a day's hunt, but some years you find none, while in others they bloom like an irrigated desert, with hundreds of grouse startling West Coast surgeons and local ranchers, who think such numbers of birds must migrate south, or "up the crick," or *somewhere* in other years. But sage grouse are not rare relics, even when they seem to disappear; they're just a feathered variety of desert forb.

The Northern Frontier District of Kenya was known to European settlers earlier in the century as the MMBA: Miles & Miles of Bloody Africa. I hereby nominate the sagelands as our version of MMBA: Miles & Miles of Blooming *Artemisia.* Early in autumn it is not a bad place to be, especially one piece I often hunt, approximately the size of Delaware if not so crowded. One stream "flows" there, by early fall usually a series of pools between dry washes, visible from two miles away as a dark snaky line of low willow and chokecherry, with an occasional lone and spindly cottonwood just turning yellow. The sage in mid-September is also tinted yellow from sagebrush blossoms, but primarily it is faded olive, underlain by the tan of prairie grasses. The closest mountains rise over the olive hills perhaps fifty miles away, islands in the sea.

In September, the hunt begins with finding water. One droughty fall (or late summer, since it was before the autumnal equinox) I sat above the biggest uncattled dam around with my twenty-gauge double, a binocular, and Gillis. It had been over ninety degrees that day, and I didn't think the ancient dog could stand the normal ten-mile hike in the heat, so we made a little two-mile walk to the hill, finding no sage grouse in the process, which was okay. There were large bird tracks in the mud around the water, mixed with pronghorn and coyote prints, and the feet that made them would be back. In the meantime, I read Tony Hillerman and talked to Gillis between pages, even though he was absolutely deaf to anything but shotgun fire. He listened anyway. Sometimes a dusty Mormon cricket stirred, and once a lonely bull mead-owlark called, too late in the year for romance, but mostly it was a silent desert wait.

The sun went down over the island mountains, and I closed the book. Gillis figured this meant it was time to hunt, and I had to point a finger in his face to make him sit again.

Soon I saw something white along the thicker sage above the dam. We only had a few minutes of legal shooting, so risking the flush of a white-tailed jackrabbit rather than a white-breasted sage bird, we walked downhill. We caught one rooster out in the open, on the dry mudflat between the sage and dam, looking at us dimly in the hope that we were indeed Angus coming to drink. No such luck. The old black dog smelled the bird and ran as best he could across the flat, and the sage grouse flew over the tall sage, wings almost touching the blossoms. At the shot his wings collapsed, and another rooster came up on the far side of the water, not quite too far for the twenty-gauge but too far for me. I missed. This didn't matter much to Gillis, who caught up to the first bird just before I did, as the wing-broken rooster tried to walk off uphill. It was a tough race between an old dog and a big grouse, but Gillis always did like the ones that were still lively when he caught them. He caught this one.

By the time we walked back down the coulee to the pickup, the stars were out. That country is one of the last places you can truly see the heavens; on clear September nights it's often hard to pick the constellations from each other. The equinox means *aurora borealis*, too, and it did this night, a pale green like a luminous accordion moving across the sky to our right. I stopped to watch and lost track of Gillis, who thirstily investigated a seephole down in the crick-bottom and got stuck. I had to rescue him, wading up to my shins in gumbo, the six-pound grouse inside the game vest bouncing around on my kidneys. I would never have found the shotgun again except for the light of stars and *borealis*. And of course I had to lift the muddy old dog into the pickup. It was a wonderful hunt, the last sage hen he ever retrieved.

(Incidentally, many natives of sage-grouse country refuse to eat them, except perhaps for the early-fall birds of the year. This is because the average Western bird hunter goes out with his full-choked pump, shoots birds on the ground or in the air, then tosses them ungutted into the back of the pickup to ride there all day with the spare tire, oil cans, and irrigating shovel. He gets home that evening and cleans the birds in the backyard, frying them immediately while his wife complains about the smell. Instead, gut your sage grouse and rinse out the body cavity within a half-hour, put them on ice in a cooler if it's a warm day, then let them age for up to a week in the bottom of the refrigerator. Even the old roosters' breasts will then be very edible, and you can make enchiladas out of their legs. Young and old taste like sage to a greater or lesser degree, but if properly cared for, the taste comes across only as a pleasant seasoning. When gutted and cooled and aged, they're something like a cross between pronghorn and dark turkey.)

My favorite time for the great sage grouse trek comes in late October or November, when the days are cool enough to make walking the undulating ridges almost like a stroll over a long suspension bridge above a pale olive bay, the mountains wearing a level slice of snow above their dusty blue. This is when sage grouse migrate. Basin-and-range birds can move as far as elk and mule deer, out of the high sage draws between the mountains down to the valleys below. Out on the high plains, they move uphill, like blue grouse in the mountains, from the tall sage along the cricks to the ridgetops. The center of the search is the high knobs cleared of sage by wind and snow, where the sage grouse dance in spring.

We hear male ruffed grouse drumming in October, or wild turkeys gobbling, reliving the rites of spring. Prairie grouse go through that autumnal hope as well. Their theory, I would guess, is if it worked once, who knows? I've even seen a few old sage roosters "booming" in the early morning along an October ridge.

You do not have to find the dancing grounds before you hunt them in fall, but if you're ever west in April, watching sage grouse in rut is much more rewarding than shopping in Billings or Casper. They puff their chest sacs and spread their tailfeathers until you can't see their feet, moving about the grassy flats like spike-hairdoed basketballs on miniature rollerskates. Once in a while they stop in front of one of the hens that wander unconcerned among them and emit a sound from their air sacs called booming, but more closely resembling (as my wife puts it) "a baby farting in a bathtub." If you get there before sunrise, a half-ton pickup in their midst makes no never mind. It all causes some wonder at the forces of evolution.

When the Blackfoot Indian poet Jim Welch first started publishing his poetry, which often forces you to feel the aridity and distance of the high plains, one of his New York editors told him it was great stuff, but sure had an awful lot of bones and wind.

That is also an accurate synopsis of sage-grouse hunting. The old dog is gone now, but there's a new brown one— almost as helpless, in different ways. Up here on the first ridge, we're gifted with the full wind, coming off sage with the melted skiff of snow from the night before, smelling like the last clean place on earth. I hike the ridgetops while the young dog circles them, both of us finding nothing in particular and everything in general. Me, perhaps a more enjoyable aerobic workout than slapping asphalt; the brown adolescent dog, certain smells that run together almost too closely, like the flavors in a bouillabaisse: mule deer, rabbitbrush, old badger hole, place-where-coyote-lifted-leg, grama grass, and the bones. Every time we leave one ridge for another, we leave the wind and find bones—of a cottontail/hawk tragedy, a winterkilled pronghorn doe, a Hereford bull bogged down in spring alkali.

And then there's another smell that makes his tail go wild and suddenly I realize a dozen sage grouse have flown, rising silently into the wind like living kites. The sound of the shot seems to be pushed back into the barrel by the wind and the last bird drops, the only one that could possibly be in range. Like the close-encounter-of-the-sage-grouse-kind with the old dog the fall before, I approach the bird just behind the young dog. He runs up to it like he has to the canvas dummies I throw in the yard and the Hungarian partridges I kill in wheat stubble, and almost grabs it before he realizes: This thing is *big*. He jumps back and barks before looking over his shoulder, as if asking me to come *deal* with this thing that smells like a wild bird but is obviously much too big. I whisper "Bring it here," and he jumps toward the bird, grabs it by the neck, and drags it ten feet before letting go, running around it twice, then grabbing it again and dragging it to me, spiked tailfeathers in the dust. "Bozo," I say, very politely, and he wags his tail as I sit on the ground and gut the bird, tossing the bitter entrails to the sage. I wipe my hands on another clump and put the bird in the game coat, then look at the new brown dog and say "Where's the birds?" He tilts his head, runs to the sage where I cleaned my hand, and sniffs, then wheels hard and looks back, saying, "I don't know, but they're around here somewhere."

Which is, of course, the answer I want, because that's the way we were headed.

3

A Simple Request

Despite the vast distances often encountered between sage grouse, one aspect of hunting them is easy: finding a place to do it. Sage grouse live on land nobody else wants, tracts of Bureau of Land Management sage and the chunks of desert homesteaders tried to farm, then abandoned to the same bureaucracy. We can just drive out there, unload the dog, load the shotgun, and go to it. Most other prairie gamebirds usually involve some knocking on doors, since they live along streams and grainfields, the cultivated parts of the Great American Desert. The places people own.

The farmhouse was rather decrepit, and when we knocked on the door nothing happened, though a pickup and car were parked outside. I looked through the door and saw stacks of old newspapers lining the walls, almost to the ceiling, and a linoleum floor with a path worn through. From somewhere beyond there came a soft creak of old floorboards. I almost knocked again, then heard another creak, and waited.

An old man came around a stack of papers, or his nose did, then an eye magnified by thick glasses. I thought he was looking to see who it was before answering the knock, but then realized he was moving, with all the speed and momentum of an out-of-control starfish, arms pumping in half-inch swings. He finally reach the door, turned the knob with both hands, and leaned backward. When the door was half-open, he suddenly leaned forward over the knob as if it were a ship's rail, glass grasshopper eyes almost touching my chin. "I don't know you," he rasped, as much challenge as statement.

I leaned back slightly, almost forgetting the name on the mailbox. "Uh, Mr. Watson? My name is John Barsness and this is my wife, Eileen, and . . ."

"What?" He leaned forward, raising a hand to one ear. I shouted my name and added, "We're from town. We wanted to know if we could hunt birds on your place."

"What?"

I shouted again. His eyebrows went up. His neck was wattled and red, and he looked like a surprised turkey dressed in Oshkosh overalls.

"Birds? Like pheasants?"

I nodded, hoping he could see me do it.

"Shoot all the goddamn pheasants you want! The sons-abitches eat my wheat, then they crap all over my haystacks. Go on down there and shoot 'em!" His face turned as red as his neck.

I nodded vigorously. "We will, as soon as the season opens."

"But don't shoot them little quails! They don't hurt nothin', and there ain't enough meat to bother with. Leave them alone, y'hear?"

I nodded, deciding against asking if he meant Huns or if he had the only wild bobwhites in Montana. The red left his face quickly, and I thought we'd better leave before he changed his mind. "Well, thanks," I said, starting to back away.

"Just a minute," he said, and I stopped. He pointed at Eileen, dressed in jeans and with a short summer haircut. "Your brother gonna hunt, too?"

My "brother," who despite her short hair and long height has other obvious features marking her as a female mammal, and I hunted Mr. Watson's place for several years, eliminating a number of vandalous pheasants, and never ran into another hunter. This was because nobody ever asked. Mr. Watson had the reputation of being an ornery old fart, as they still say in the more rural areas of the West, and nobody else dared. We were new in town and didn't know any better.

We asked Mr. Watson for permission to hunt his over-grown half-section (bad farming but good pheasanting) a full month before the season opened, following the first and most important of the standard rules of asking to hunt—do it early, before anybody else, preferably in the slack time between planting and harvest. The theory is that farmers will then be mellow, beneficent, and neighborly, willing to share the bounteous wildlife they hold so dear. Just like Mr. Watson.

There are a number of other rules that various authorities have formulated over the years, to wit:

Two: Don't ask at six in the morning on opening day.

Three: Shave, shower, and dress in clean clothes.

Four: Don't go to the door en masse, since five men dressed in hunting clothes might frighten isolated farm folk.

Five: If the landowner hesitates, offer to do chores in exchange for hunting.

Six: If given permission, share some of the bounty of the hunt.

Perhaps it is the times we live in, my skeptical nature, or many meetings with stewards of the land like Mr. Watson, but I have begun to have my doubts.

One year Eileen and I hunted with two friends who had invited us over to the big wheat country north of Great Falls for opening day of pheasant season. We arrived at a farmhouse door just at dawn. No, our pals did not have permission to hunt, though they'd hunted this particular farm before. Number One Friend went to knock on the door, wearing a pair of torn coveralls that hadn't been washed since the season before. A youngish man came to the door, wearing a T-shirt and pajama bottoms, rubbing his eyes. We watched the conversation, dogs whining in their boxes behind the rear seat of the Blazer.

"That isn't the same guy," Number Two Friend said. The man they'd gotten permission from some years before had been elderly.

Number One Friend came back and said the old landowner had died (a good reason not to ask too long before hunting season) but the new owner, despite being awakened before sunrise with a hangover, had said to go ahead. He also asked, as he looked over at the Blazer, "Why didn't your friends get out with you? They got a social disease?"

So much for Rules One, Two, Three, and Four.

Rules Five and Six take sense to operate. Farmers and ranchers have enough trouble these days without some stockbroker offering to buck haybales. If you are a stockbroker and somebody lets you hunt, give him some market tips. Most older farmers play the futures game. It turned out that Mr. Watson's stacks of newspapers were all old *Wall Street Journals*, and he owned half the municipal water systems of northern Montana. Like most farmers who lived through the Depression, he simply didn't spend any money he didn't have to.

Also, many country folk do not eat wild game, or only certain species. I took a couple of West Coast friends out a few years back, to the country along a remote but permanent prairie stream, but I could hunt only a day before getting back to work. They knocked on a few doors afterward and got permission to hunt one place that had four kinds of birds:

Huns, pheasants, sage, and sharptailed grouse. They had the good instincts to offer the ranch wife a couple of pheasants, withholding the "wilder" birds. This not only got them permission to hunt "any old time they wanted," but an invitation to dinner.

Most of the time, it also helps to have the birds frypan ready before you give them away. These days, most ranch wives are as used to plastic-wrapped chicken and steak as any Long Island supermarket shopper. A feathered pheasant is not only a public-relations goof, but a practical problem to a microwave chef.

There are exceptions. One old bachelor rancher, whose land I frequently hunt and fish, loves all wild game, especially birds, which he prefers to pluck himself. I present him with gutted trout and pheasants, and he lets me have the run of the place.

What it all boils down to is that there are no hard-and-fast rules. One November my friend Fred and I drove up and down the Bitterroot River, asking at every likely looking farm. The first place had a new four-wheel-drive, the type that only people who've moved from the city drive. It also had Ohio plates. We should have known better, but knocked anyway. A very good-looking red-haired woman answered the door, leaving the chain hooked and speaking to us in whispers. Her husband wasn't home, and they had horses we might shoot. She looked at us as if she might be next in line. Fred, a native Montanan who grew up in a small logging town where everybody hunted on everybody else's land, beat his head steadily on the pickup's window as we drove away.

At the next place an old woman gave us a lecture about somebody shooting one of her calves. From the story, it might have been Butch and Sundance.

By then it was almost evening so we stopped at the next place down the road. A middle-aged man, who looked like Walter Mitty, came to the door and said sure, but there were already a couple of guys hunting. So I asked if we could hunt in the morning and he said fine, and told us where to park our pickup. I asked if he wanted us to stop by the house again before we hunted, and he said no, he'd recognize our outfit.

The next morning we drove down there and parked by the gate where he'd told us, let the dog out, and started hunting. Before we'd gone a hundred yards, we heard a door slam in the house, a quarter mile away, and saw a large person jump in a pickup and come roaring our way. We walked back to our pickup in time to greet a woman who, as Fred later put it, "would field-dress around two-fifty." She was the wife, and she was mad. She had a thirty-thirty in her hands and was going to call the sheriff. We finally got her calmed down enough to explain that her husband had given us permission, but she never calmed down enough to let us hunt. He'd gone to Billings and "never mentioned a word about it."

So who the hell knows? You can't account for dysfunctional marriages, calves rustled sixty years ago, or someone's taste in bird feathers. Clean clothes might offend some old populist from North Dakota. Some people actively hate pheasants. I once ran into a stylish woman who looked exactly like Barbara Stanwyck and asked me in for brandy and hors d'oeuvres. This was back along a sagebrush road where people drove seventy miles to town for "supplies," usually once a month. After several experiences like that, and decades of knocking on farmhouse doors, I have found only one rule that works with any certainty: Get as far away from cities as you can.

Another friend and I had been living in my pickup camper for three days, up in the lonely country along the Saskatchewan border. We looked and probably smelled bad. When we asked to hunt the bottomlands of a farm thirty miles up a gravel road, they told us to park in the farmyard and plug into their electricity. They invited us to dinner, and one of the sons wanted to show us where the pheasants lived, but his father told him he better get his chores done. That night we all drank some beer together and a day later, laden with pheasants, we were invited back the next year.

Close to town, nobody gets to hunt, except parish priests, family doctors, or in-laws. But back in the hinterlands, many folks are glad to have some company. They may offer brandy and canapes, or beer and chips, or simply their birds and land. If they don't, they simply aren't sociable, and their neighbors will be doubly glad to see you, even if you wear dirty coveralls, bring your brother, or have a social disease.

4

A Tale of Two Pheasants

In these delicate times, people who actually deal with fish, birds or mammals before all edible parts are wrapped in plastic are looked on either as half-wits, unable to learn the secrets of silicon chips or mutual funds and so pull themselves up from working on a fishing boat or at the meat counter, or barbarians who enjoy killing wild creatures in the same way Attila liked to rape and pillage. As a consequence, it has become fashionable among our more "sensitive" hunters and anglers to regret the passing of any wild creature, not just once and quietly in the woods, but many times and weeping, in print. I have probably overdone some of this myself, but have retained enough sense of balance to keep from releasing every trout I catch or proclaim, as one ultrasensitive did at a recent party, that he had given up shooting anything that was red meat. Perhaps the next step will be shotshells loaded with dozens of tiny paint capsules, so we can claim a "kill" when a Day-Glo orange splash (biodegradable, of course) hits a grouse in the tailfeathers.

All of which has something to do with the confession about to be made. As Tom McGuane once put it, I do not feel exactly hunky-dory when game goes down. But when the game is an old cock pheasant that was born in the wild, and has wintered at least once in the land of blizzards and foxes, I can also feel a certain measure of inordinate glee.

The reason is, of course, that such mature wild pheasants have forced me to play catch-and-release bird hunting too many times. I know there are probably a lot of you out there who earnestly believe that pheasants are too easy to shoot, or even too easy to flush in easy range. I have met many of you in my time, and usually just nod my head and grin like a barbarian when you recite tales of how your Brittany pointed umpteen birds one morning and you and all your buddies filled out before noon. I am not talking about those pheasants, the ones born in barns on game preserves, or on hunting leases shot only twice a season, or young roosters surrounded in opening-day cornfields. I am talking old birds, with spurs as big as a two-year-old turkey gobbler's, on land that has been hunted, not just shot. I am talking thorn-thicket pheasants, cattail pheasants, alder-swamp pheasants that have never seen a cornfield, that will either run when they hear a pickup door close at a quarter-mile, or hold until they know you're on the other side of the willows and then take off too low for any radar. Who, if they did meet your tender Brittany down there in the thick and shadowy might just haul off and kick her in the teeth with those elongated spurs.

I love to kill those pheasants and eat their savage breasts.

It was the best of times; it was the worst of times. Today we could chase pheasants, but on the morrow we could not, for the season would be closed.

It was mid-December, and sun shone on the rounded white domes of the limestone mountains to the southwest, and also shone down here along the creekbottom of Arnie's ranch, a two-mile stretch of alder and willow swamp, rose-bush bends, and cattail thickets that had been hunted over the previous seven weeks not just by me and my wife and our eight-month-old chocolate Labrador, but by every local kid possessing a break-action four-ten. Arnie is our local county commissioner, a seventy-year-old rancher who once went to law school Back East, who, when I bring him a couple of Hungarian partridge on an October afternoon and say that I've already cleaned them, nods and smiles, ashes flicking off the filterless Camel in his hand, and says, "You're a gentleman and a scholar."

Arnie lets everybody hunt.

Actually, I had not hunted Arnie's seriously for pheasants since opening week, when I killed three or four young roosters, the first my young dog had ever seen, finding them out along the edges of the knee-high wild roses where he could snuffle along on that new and intriguing smell until the young dumb bird would fly and I would shoot it where the young dumb dog could see it fall. Out there, in that low and wimpy cover, we had some fine adventures and circuitous retrieves, Keith sometimes dropping the big loose warm thing four or five times before finally bringing it to my feet—but needing only to find two birds before he got the idea: to chase that funny smell until a bird flew, and then land with a loud sound where he could slobber on it.

We kept hunting the edges of the bottoms, finding a few Huns, and the prairies farther back, finding Huns and sharp-tails and sage grouse, but I avoided the real heart of the bottoms after the first few young birds had been killed. When we had the general bird-scent well ingrained into the new memory cells, and he had put on a few more pounds of brush-muscle, we went back down there, pushing harder into the willows and cattails and alders. In about two trips he caught onto the fact that the animals—deer, birds, jackrabbits, foxes, whatever—lived in the thick stuff. When I hand-signaled him into a certain thicket, he skirted it for thirty yards, then crashed down there and circled back toward me. My God, I thought, a natural. Of course he chased some deer and foxes and an occasional bird too far. I let him, at first, then started stopping him. Soon he was stopping himself. Well, most of the time.

Today would be graduation, the serious search for the old outlaw pheasants that live, like wild longhorn steers down in the Texas Brush Country, in the thickest, thorniest, darkest shadows for almost all their lives. In this quest Keith and I asked Eileen to come along, since she had recently graduated from the mere killing of whitetails and elk to shooting birds on the wing. It helps to have two hunters along with the dog down in the bottoms, for the best way to work things in most of the cover is to have one hunter on each side of the creek's meander. The cover grows on the inside of each river bend; the dog works between the hunters, crossing the water to each patch of cover. The birds tend to flush across the water, away from the hunter they hear walking through the rose-bushes bordering their alder bunkers. It's the job of the hunter in the open to guess where the dog is in all that inter-woven willow and alder, and run hard along the outside of the bend to keep up, to be in the right place to intercept the flight of a flushed outlaw. It is a problem of intuitive guess-work, complicated by running parabolas up and down steep banks, side coulees full of old tractor parts, barbedwire, and occasional whitetailed deer whose first crash automatically brings the double gun up.

The very first bend got Keith excited. He entered from my side of the creek, and then a red fox went out the other end, low along the ground beside the creekbank. Keith bent so many trees in there, trying to get his ninety pounds after the fox, that for a moment he could have been one of Arnie's old Hereford cows. Then he pushed his chest through one last lattice of willows and loped on the fox-trail for six steps before standing and almost pointing, then looking back at me.

"Birds," I said. "We are hunting birds."

The next two bends held nothing except enough alders to tire him slightly, so that he didn't run skull on into so many big alders. Then we entered the swamp.

I do not know whether you have hunted many swamp pheasants. It's much like hunting ruffed grouse where most of the thorns are replaced by gaseous mud. You pull on Maine Hunting Shoes or even hipboots and circle rather aimlessly around in there, thinking maybe you'll put up a bird quickly and get this high adventure over with, and then, within a half-hour, ceasing to care. By then you're drinking sweat and have fallen once or twice, if you're among the more agile and lucky. When a bird does go out, it is just like shooting ruffed grouse in their thicker coverts, except that half the time your feet are anchored by Devonian muck and you've got to hit that pheasant much harder. I like an ounce-and-a-quarter of fives, even at fifteen yards. If they don't fall dead, even a very good dog won't find them. This particular swamp was built by beavers, who dammed up the main channel and then, once it filled and diverted the creek to an old meander, dammed that too, creating a marshy peninsula three hundred yards long that can be pentrated only by wading the shallow water at the upper end.

So we slopped around in there, putting up a blue heron, keeping track of each other by the sounds of cracking brush, or cursing, or occasional glimpses of blaze orange, the hats on our heads and Keith's collar. We pushed down toward the end of the peninsula, between the two dams, and cornered six hens that flew right into the sun, me hollering, "Hen-hen-hen!" like some barbarian half-wit trying to sell chickens in a swamp, and Eileen shouting back, "What what what?!" and Keith crashing and snuffling like a hungry boar after animated truffles.

This was Eileen's first adventure in the swamp, and after we'd extricated ourselves, she said, "You expect me to shoot those things in there?"

At the third bend beyond the swamp, I was trotting hard along the barren bank when Keith put up the first rooster. I could hear the dog wrestling with the thicker brush, the stuff that gives and then grabs as tightly as an old wicker chair whose seat suddenly collapses, sucking you down through the busted innards. Even Keith is not so enthused with willow-claustrophobia to go into that stuff without a reason, so I ran and saw the bird thrash its way out of the willowtops, and then Keith's head emerge as he pulled like a Percheron in harness against the brush. The rooster crossed sixty yards out, and then a hen right behind him. I stood and watched as they sailed toward a line of willows growing along an old cut-off river channel a quarter-mile away, marking where the rooster sat down near a young cottonwood. Keith came across the creek, diving and then churning through a pool and then hauling himself, glistening like an otter, up the cutbank, watching hard toward where the birds had gone.

Eileen appeared beyond the end of the brush, on the far side of the creek. "Come on across," I said. "We have them surrounded." She found a shallow riffle. Keith ran toward her and bounded through the shallows, hopping up on his hind legs beside her as if she'd disappeared for a week.

We stood and contemplated the distant line of willows. "I think," I said, "that you should take Keith and go in at the left end, near those three cottonwoods, and I'll circle around to the right and find a place to stand in the brush. He'll probably stick to the brush, and if you don't get a shot, I might."

She nodded, and we took off in our separate ellipses. Every once in a while I would look back at the two new bird-hunters, both growing smaller very quickly across the open grassland, the brown dog always wanting to charge ahead, his tail circling, prancing as he heeled beside her. I hurried ahead and came to the edge of the willows, a twenty-foot band growing hard against a high cutbank, and found a gap in the brush behind a pair of big chokecherry bushes, where the wild roses opened for a bit and I could see the ground (if he ran) and could also shoot to right or left if he flew. I opened the Spanish double and checked the loads, then waited.

Soon I heard a shot, and Eileen shouted, "He's coming your way." I put my right foot back slightly, and a pheasant appeared in the air between the two chokecherry bushes, just over head-high, and saw me. Eileen said later that even from a hundred yards she could see him say "Oh, *no*," and try to backpedal, like a cartoon pheasant scrabbling for purchase on linoleum air. From my end I could see the same bird-thought, but almost above my head; since he really could not fly backward, try as he might, he veered to my right over the cutbank and under the sun, where I swung hard and shot with the open barrel as the muzzles crossed his neck. He twirled slowly in a silhouetted pinwheel, a dozen feathers hanging in the sunlight, and fell absolutely dead perhaps twelve yards away, in the shallow dry channel where I thought he might run.

It felt wonderful.

I waited for Eileen and Keith. When he came bounding up, frantic with shots being fired, I made him heel and then signaled him toward the bird. He grabbed it gleefully, half-tossing it into the air after he picked it up, and then dancing around me once with his neck arched and eyes watching me over the big bird, before bringing it to my hand.

It was indeed a big old bird, the spurs as long as a two-year-old gobbler's, but several times as sharp. The tailfeathers hung almost to my knees as I held him in my hands, looking at his feathers.

Eileen said, "That was *great*."

"It takes two people and a dog to outmaneuver one pheasant."

She looked at him, thinking. "You want to hunt some more?"

He was too perfect to ruin by going on. "No. This one is enough." Even Keith seemed to think so, panting and sniffing at the bird. Not wanting to let the pheasant out of our sight, I carried him by the legs rather than putting him in my game coat. We left the bottoms and crossed a fence up to the winter wheatfields, and could see the pickup parked three-quarters of a mile away across the flat green-lined earth. We started walking in the December afternoon, the light turning yellow as the sun moved down toward the mountains.

We walked within thirty yards of the next fenceline before the covey of Hungarian partridge got up, six small birds whirring and then angling to the left, in front of Eileen. Out of the hunting mode, she just looked, but I dropped our pheasant and raised the double gun—then realized I couldn't swing toward the covey because my wife stood in front of me.

"Why didn't you shoot?" I said.

"I didn't realize they were Huns at first," she said. I shrugged and bent down to pick up the pheasant, and that's when the second rooster took off from the low wheatgrass along the fenceline, just to the right of where the partridges had been, flying to my side. I straightened up and swung hard, feeling slow and late, shooting with the modified barrel and missing, realizing as I missed that he was closer than I thought, then hitting him solidly with the second barrel as he began to veer away slightly. He fell at an angle that exactly complemented the angle of his rise, landing with a whump like a punted football on the far side of a cross-fence. Keith left a clump of brown hair on the barbwire, then picked up the bird and again performed his victory dance, as if he had put the pheasant up from the darkest thicket of the swamp. It was a match of the first bird, right down to the length and shape of its spurs.

"Now can we quit?" I asked. Eileen nodded. The two big birds almost balanced the weight of the Spanish gun in my other hand as we walked across the soft brown-green field. We had accidentally caught the second rooster out for his brief feed, and we would never have gotten close to him if we hadn't come up from the bottom at the exact angle we had, with the line of wheatgrass along the fence just at the curve of the hill. We had acquired one old pheasant as a result of hard work and low cunning, and the other by the purest sort of luck. This is, of course, very much like the rest of our lives, which can at times be as fine as old pheasants falling from the air.

5

Hungarian

It is now the in thing to come west and chase Hungarian partridge each fall. They're the particular favorite of bird hunters who, for lack of a better (or even vaguely applicable) word, must be termed yuppies. These folks use the term "world class" to define anything from restaurants to bird hunting. Because of their interest in Western fun, a few good restaurants now exist out here. Rather than deride this change (as many of my fellow natives do), I compliment yuppie bird hunters on their good taste in dining and gamebirds. The first creates options other than beefsteak, and my yuppie friends are willing to let me hunt partridge over their pointing dogs, some of which are almost trained.

The Hun is indeed fun to hunt. It's a covey bird, so bonded to its siblings that the flush resembles a cluster-bomb—if cluster-bombs were made of small red ruffed grouse, and ruffed grouse lived on the treeless plains. Huns live on the prairies, where we wiped out the native grass and hence the native birds, and there never have been many poplars and brambles to spoil the horizon. This appeals greatly to immigrant hunters used to flushing two unseen ruffed grouse a weekend, who have read Havilah Babcock and Robert Ruark and haven't a chance in quail-hunter's heaven of getting invited to shoot bobwhite on a big plantation.

It is very pleasant to hunt Hungarians with an immigrant out for a few days with his shock-collared pointing dogs, those with the bloodlines reaching back to the Roadrunner. Let 'em loose and walk along through the stubble, discussing the latest fiction in *The New Yorker* or where to have pasta that night. This method is quite relaxing to the host, since the guest ends up doing all the shouting and shocking. Buy him dinner at a trendy restaurant and it's a square deal all around, even if you have walked him fourteen miles, chasing Huns in circles.

Hun-hunter's lore has it that a covey, if chased far enough, returns to the original spot. The trick is to be able to track them through the air. On cloudy days, a good pair of binoculars would help to separate small birds from large landscape at a half-mile or more. This thought first occurred to me a decade ago, but has never recurred at the right time, such as when holding a shotgun while an impatient dog dances at the front door.

But even with the unassisted eye, frightened Huns can be tracked for long distances. My personal record is over two miles, measured on a topo map. A yuppie friend from the Midwest named Steve brought his Brittany out one October and we hunted a ranch north of town. The ranch is bisected by an abandoned railroad. This makes for interesting walking, since aside from miles of arid landscape, you have to cross two barbwire fences and the steep roadbed if you want to hunt each side of the ranch. We headed out into the grain-stubble wilderness, toward an old windmill and barn. Beyond the barn rose tan hills occasionally topped by the metallic lavender of cheatgrass, and then low-strung mountains, like the top of a new wave.

The hatch had been sparse that year, and we'd walked a mile of stubble and were in the grass when the dog turned suddenly as if he'd dropped his wallet, staring at the ground behind him. It took a while but eventually we realized he was on point. The covey flushed at the far edge of improved-cylinder and Steve killed one, and then we watched them fly. They flew toward the old railroad and then over it, and I could still barely see them against the far yellow field when they sideslipped toward the ground.

It took most of an hour to get there, and a little while later the dog pointed more conventionally. When we walked in together one bird got up. It was an easy straightaway, and when Steve shot it the rest of the covey rose, headed back toward where they came. I killed another and then we watched them pitch over the railroad. I looked at Steve. He is that rarity, a round yuppie (he *really* likes our New West restaurants), used to working little five-acre woods for ruffed grouse, not two-mile fields. He shrugged. We hiked over, crossed one fence, climbed the rail grade, crossed the second fence, and the dog pointed. This time the birds let us walk among them before they flew. We picked up three, and then Steve allowed as he'd had enough Montana bird-chasing for the day.

They hold closer on successive flushes, tired by the flight. In high school one of my girlfriends was the very young daughter of a very old Polish aristocrat, who had fled Europe just before the Communist curtain. In his younger days, he said, they rode after partridge on horseback, chasing the coveys across the plains of Poland until the birds were so exhausted they could be caught by hand and placed in the saddlebags. My own (bipedal) record is four flushes, only the last close enough for a shot. They came up at my feet, from the same bend in the wild rosebushes they'd flushed wild from an hour before.

Another trait endearing Huns to quail-plantation wannabes is the home life of each covey. Like bobwhites, Huns tend to live in the same general area and can be relocated by persistent hunters. This was first pointed out by the old Sioux Indian who, at the time was my grandfather-in-law. Before one hunt on the Reservation, we had to take a load of junk to the local landfill, and he told me to have my shotgun handy on the way. "We might run into those Huns that live by the dump road," he said, and we did. During the three years I lived on the Reservation, perhaps a dozen members of the Dump Road Covey graced my table.

(Ben had many stories concerning the wildlife of the plains, going all the way back to when the first white home-steaders reached South Dakota. He said his grandfather's people laughed at the settlers, with their slow cattle and foolish birds. Why herd such creatures, when buffalo and prairie chickens were there for the taking? But in a few years the last buffalo were gone, and the prairie chickens disap-peared as quickly as the land was plowed. By the time Ben was young, the white folks were releasing Huns and pheasants to replace the native birds. These European gamebirds thrived on the European grain that now covered the prairie, and Ben hunted them hard. As Sitting Bull said, "When the buffalo are gone, we will hunt mice, for we are hunters and we want our freedom.")

I try to invite friends like Steve out at least once a year, but I grew up in world far from quail fantasies, To tell the truth, walking along and yakking while the dogs do the hunting makes me vaguely uncomfortable after a day or so. Most of my personal Hun hunting involves (of course) a Labrador retriever, the same dog that catches doves and geese and pheasants on other fall days, and walking out where I know the address and work schedule of each covey. We hunt together, the bring-back dog and I, feeling our way into the time of day, the wind and temperature, how the wheat harvest went this year, and how recently we last found the Tractor Grave Covey, the one that lives near the abandoned John Deere. We work the irrigation ditches in hot September, the fence corners and field edges on mid-October evenings, and the lee sides of shelterbelts and old homesteads after the snow falls. Sometimes when we get a little dreamy, we quarter a strip of stubble; but for the most part we scour the little places biologists like to call "microhabitat," partridge islands in the waves of grass.

The last time we did this along the edge of Arnie's lower field. Two coveys live there, and one is the Brush Covey. Huns are not supposed to like tall cover, but this bunch does, heading directly for the pheasant stuff along the creek at any faint threat of dog. I have flushed both Brush and Bench Coveys within fifteen minutes of each other, and one always heads downhill into the willows, the other across the open stubble toward Poland.

The best way to catch the Brushers is to work the edges of the creekbottom cover first. So we did, the big dog plowing over alders like an erratic D8 Caterpillar. Then we crossed the lower fence and worked the wild rosebushes in the bottom. I was convinced we had missed them when they rose from the grass and came for my head like a herd of flying squirrels. I got the double up quickly and killed the lead bird, splitting the covey before they beat me to death with their primaries. This made the day a quick triumph, so we celebrated by letting the dog scare all the trout in that bend of the creek.

Wet and refreshed, we headed up to the low river terrace where the wheatfield starts. Huns like these places, the gentle shoulders of the prairie where they can loaf about in head-high grass, able to go whichever way the wind blows—and out here it always blows. We walked a mile of creek-shoulder before we put up the Bench birds, just out of range. I watched them put down a half-mile away, right in the middle of a wheat strip. We moved into the wind, the dog quartering to each side of the narrow strip, and when he smelled the birds he stood still for one illuminated second, and then moved forward cautiously, nose sucking air like a small bellows. He moved two steps to the side, then one to the left, chasing that curl of odor, and then more certainly for another fifty feet before the covey came up. I was as ready as any racehorse and missed the first shot by shooting in front of the lead bird, then relaxed and slowed and killed two with the second barrel, quite by accident. One fell dead, and the other wingbeat twice in the wheat before the dog pounced like a hundred-pound terrier.

I did not watch the rest of the birds fly off. We had three, and that seemed enough from personal coveys, despite the generous limits the state decrees. We walked the half-mile back to the creek, where the dog drank after his toils, and I cleaned the little gray-brick birds. Beyond us was the horizon, uncluttered by trees, in the distance a squared butte asking us to step on over and see whether Huns lived there, in the foothills or beyond. That's the vision that often arrives at the same instant as the food in those restaurants at the end of the day, when the herbed pasta stops halfway to my mouth and I'm suddenly up to my shell loops in Huns again, which seems as good a way as any to fill the memory banks. I have forgotten some world-class restaurants, but even my ponderous Labrador of a memory can still retrieve each partridge that ever flew across the shortgrass prairie sky.

6

Other Spaces, Other Farms

Bird hunting has always been connected in my mind with the clank of automatic pig feeders, the result of spending my first hard-core shooting season in the employ (five bucks a day, room, board, most Sundays off) of the Sixty-Six Quarter-Circle Ranch, which covers twenty square miles of upland habitat near the Yellowstone River in eastern Montana. I was sixteen, an impressionable age, and the routine was to get up before dawn and fix coffee while other hunters—neighbors, mostly, with a few city cousins mixed in—arrived in pickup trucks. A white fence surrounded the lawn of the two-story ranch house, and beyond stood about thirty feeders scattered among three hundred pigs, the aluminum doors keeping a constant backbeat to the barks of the ranch dog as he greeted neighbors. If you listened closely, standing on the plank porch and shivering in the September half-light, you might hear a coyote talk back from the grassy ridge to the east, where you were about to go and slay sharptailed grouse.

My second connection is of coffee falling in my lap as the ranch pickup bounced up the coyote ridge. By the time we topped out along the first tableland stubblefield, perhaps one sip had made my mouth, and folks in the other trucks seemed in the same fix. Even at sixteen, the ranch kitchen seemed a more stable drinking platform, but kids don't question unshaven Stetsoned veterans of the sharptail ridges.

The strategy involved driving the field edges until we saw the dark heads of grouse rising above the stubble like gallinaceous periscopes. The image that comes to mind is of an elongated shadow, a Ford pickup stretched across a field by the barely risen sun, the most intense light around our heads in the cab, creating a halo that danced along with our shadows on the slick stalks. Behind the halo another shadow bounced back and forth like a flop-eared Ping-Pong ball—the ranch dog, a basset hound who loved to chase both pronghorns and birds, rarely catching either, but always making them move. Behind us other long shadows carried other troops.

Then one truck would stop in a dust cloud and everyone would pile out, men and dogs and kids and shotguns and thermos bottles, and take off in a long line across the stubble. Of course the birds often flushed far out of shotgun range, alternately flapping and sailing against the distant pale-lit ridges. Perhaps one or two would hold tightly, rising anywhere but my part of the line, so I'd see the bird come out of the stubble at an acute angle, then obliquely fall. After a one-beat pause came the sound of the distant shot, just as some dark dog-shadow grabbed the fallen grouse and then did a fair imitation of a demented figure skater, running and circling, performing parallelograms and figure-eights while a distant cowboy shouted. This may startle some people, but I have known men who could train the most efficient cutting horses in a county whose bird dogs didn't know the word "come."

By the time we reached the end of the second field, where the table dropped off into grama grass, yucca, occasional junipers, rattlesnake rocks, and rosebushed draws, the sun stood full and we could feel the heat cutting the dew on the dust. The birds scuttled downhill, under the shady roses, through tunnels they'd forced over the summer. We'd split up so two or three men and one dog could work each draw, the sharptails rising closely now, in singles and small bunches, the twenty-gauge seeming more plausible in my hands. Halfway down, where sage joined the roses in some coulees, sage grouse turned up, wings seeming as broad as those of the buteo hawks we could see turning on the morning thermals. Farther down, along the old irrigation ditch that ran along the base of the hills, we might put up a few young cock pheasants, feathers just turning to their mature colors, and remember the place for October. Or a covey of Hungarian partridge rising too fast for big-grouse reactions. To the north, the flat-topped rimrock ridges looked crewcut under ponderosa and juniper, and some sprung-hipped ranchhand would vow something about a turkey hunt in the afternoon.

To the north the cottonwooded Yellowstone meandered through the flat valley, corn and sugar-beet fields surrounding the trees almost too green to be believed from our vantage of dust and cactus.

When we reached the barbwire border of the Sixty-Six Quarter Circle, just below the ditch, the youngest hands (make a guess) would be privileged to run back up the hill to the pickups and drive down the dusty ridges to the veterans, half-asleep against sandstone blocks fallen from the rimmed hill above. Then we'd return to the cool house and eat eggs and bacon made from the brothers and sisters of the pigs still working the aluminum trapdoors out back. Maybe someone had killed a rattler, and we'd cook that up for supper, along with the chicken-fried birds. It wasn't until quite a bit later that I realized this wasn't the farm-country bird hunting all those guys in *Outdoor Life* wrote about, and never would be.

You can tell when you've left those other farms behind. Just cross the Missouri River at Chamberlain, South Dakota, or Bismarck in the north, or any of the smaller highways between. To the east, in the rearview mirror, the land is flatter, filled with new kettlehole lakes where one of the recent glaciers lived. Through the curved windshield to the west, everything grows suddenly raw and eroded, and filled with strange beasts. Black-and-white magpies float like unbalanced toy gliders over diamond willow fenceposts, and pronghorns float far more gracefully over badlands hills.

The geological and zoological differences show up in us, too. The people wear bigger hats, and though the major riverbottoms can resemble the Midwest—farms close together with corn between—up above those rivers you can get out of sight of humanity and stay that way for long stretches. The land can change from cattails to cactus to ponderosa in a few miles, and the agriculture is likewise "diversified," as the landowners like to say. My wife, raised in New York City and for fifteen years an urban Montanan, found out about this during a conversation in a bar in our small town.

"So are you farmers or ranchers?" she finally asked, trying to pin down one of the diversified. He shrugged, showing a Copenhagen grin. "Then you must be farchers," she said.

The farchers grow some cows and small grains and maybe a little something else. A few years back one family along the Canadian border, hard-pressed to meet the mortgage, put up some bales of marijuana. They had just about gotten caught up with the bank, too, when the local authorities intervened. But the mixture usually runs from corn to wheat to malting barley, from pigs to sheep to beef cattle, depending on where you are between the Missouri bottoms and the face of the Rockies. The mixture of birds varies, too; but as a general rule, sage grouse appear only occasionally on the true farms, with sharptails best in the prime dryland wheat country, along with the most Huns, and both pheasants and Huns close to the "cricks" and rivers. With the exception of sage birds, you're more likely to find good hunting on the farms, instead of the yellow squares on the Bureau of Land Management maps, the public domain that gets pounded so hard by private cattle. But you're also likely to run into occasional signs saying "No Bird Hunting—This Year—There Aren't Enough," even though you've just seen four coveys of Huns along the ditches. To many farchers, "bird" and "pheasant" are synonyms.

Five whole weeks into the season one fall, Eileen and I asked at the first house out of one of those one-bar, one-elevator towns, and found that nobody had hunted the farm all fall. Since there were more Huns in that county than there are boiled peanuts in Georgia, we put up more coveys than we could keep track of from the flat stubble. We'd taken eight birds in about an hour, and then the dog put up a pheasant from along a little crick. When he folded dead at my first shot, it seemed too good to be true.

It was. The farcher looked mournfully at the bird when I showed it to him after the hunt. "Don't have many of them," he said. Since 98 percent of the place was level wheatfields, this made sense, but many farchers believe that pheasants are spontaneously generated from old stubble and overgrazed pastures. He didn't care whether we hunted his Huns into oblivion (which we had no desire to do), but he liked his pheasants live.

On other farms, I've been asked to do small favors. "Yeah, you can hunt pheasants," the guy said as we stood out by his machine shed, where he was repairing a combine header. "As long as you shoot some of those whitetails eatin' my winter wheat." Since wheat deer taste good, and you could buy several tags that overpopulated year, this seemed fair. Especially since there were six pheasants feeding among his pigs, two hundred yards away.

On one ranch I hunted for several falls, the small creek wound by the house, bordered by up to fifty feet of roses, alders, willows, cattails, and cottonwoods. Bordering the brush were alfalfa and barley fields. Pheasants liked this. In good years, the shooting was far better than any I've had in the cornfield Midwest. We'd send two guys down the creek with a dog or two, posting a third at the next opening in the brush, usually by one of the log bridges between fields. All you had to do was walk up to within fifty yards of the blocker and stand there. Some of the birds tried to run through the knee-high wheatgrass, the crested tops waving above the birds, but they all flew when they reached the short stubble.

There was another farm where early in the year Huns held along a small irrigation ditch, and if Gillis put them up wild the first time, they'd just dive back in farther along the grassy banks. The second time they'd come up less than a shotgun length away, and two and sometimes three would fall in the hot dust of the fallow fields alongside. Later on we grew to know the exact fence corners where each covey held, and when they entered the fields each evening, and took it upon ourselves to be there each day after my work and Gillis's afternoon nap.

But despite those two tracts of heaven, my best thoughts of farm country come from north of the Missouri, the edges of the rolling river valleys of far northern Montana and southern Saskatchewan. Up there the rainless strip east of the Rockies ends far to the west, and the coulees grow more cover than the hot plains farther south. Dryland wheat grows better up there, too, on the glacier-flattened hilltops above the coulees. It's best to get there in hot September, when the few cottonwoods around the springs have just begun to turn. Anyone who thinks the plains barren and monochromatic has never seen the metallic lavender of cured cheatgrass merge into the green and rust and pointillist yellows of the fall coulees, with the white-yellow wheat stubble and wisped clouds above turning in that enormous sky.

By the time I'd found these truly northern plains, I'd realized there was no good reason to get up at dawn and look for grouse heads in the stubble. Instead the routine turned into civilized breakfasts and a daylight drive ending at the edge of a lonely plateau during that transition between dawn and hot midday. This meant the grouse had already filled their crops with waste grain and wandered into the shade of ash and roses and chokecherries below. Instead of stretching their necks to watch several fools advance across the wide-open stubble, they'd be stuffed and lazy and content, just the right sort of birds for a lay-a-bed hunter.

The last time I found them was too long ago, when most bird hunts take place. A friend and I parked my old Bronco three hundred yards from where we expected the birds to be, and let Gillis run off his morning zappiness while we loaded our guns. Except for the prickly stubble beneath our feet, and a long barbwire fence a mile away across the river valley, we might have been hunting in buffalo time. There were no farmhouses between cornfields, or indeed any sense of that squared order we like to impose on irregular curves. Instead the coulees dropped in green-rusty dendritic paths, the upper fingers reaching toward us, the lower arms joining the slow river. Two miles away, on the other side of the valley, the sandy yellow faces of plateaus the exact height of our vantage point seemed like a natural mirror, reflecting at a speed much slower than light, as if we gazed at a somewhat distant past.

Gillis put his nose into the damp wheat and snorted. We walked to the edge and looked into the big patch of gray-green buffalo-berry below, the thorns shiny between the orange berries. Gillis looked at me, and I said, "Go on, get 'em." As he picked a route between the thorns we heard birds running in dry leaves. Then the brushtops vibrated in odd places, and one bird came out straight up, almost still in the air. We both shot and the bird disappeared, loose feathers drifting downhill, and three more birds came up through them. The main covey went up—maybe ten birds—and we shot some more, and then the stragglers at odd moments, when we were bent to take birds from the dog or reloading.

They all scattered down through the mile-long coulee, dropping into the taller brush at each bend, two birds into a patch of chokecherries, one into some thick roses, three into some more buffalo-berry, others sailing so far we couldn't hear their distant *clutlutlutl*. I took the last dead bird from Gillis and twisted my arm to slide it into my vest, and thought: *Well, this should be fun, like a trout stream with deep holes at each bend, with a prairie trout or two lying in each shadow, waiting to fly.* And that is exactly the way it was: each curve of the dry river a place where you could pause for a moment and think—before something foreordained happened in ways not quite exactly imagined—of all the things that mattered most, at least, right then. Which is far more than you can expect in some other places I've been.

7

Riley's Birds

The barbed-wire gate opened easily, and I thought: God bless lonely Irish ranchers. Riley didn't run as many cattle now that his wife had moved to town with the two boys, and hardly ran anything on this sandy barren sage, so his gates were all relaxed, unlike Riley. As I opened the gate a jackrabbit, already winter white, jumped from behind a fencepost and bounded across the sagebrush flat, the land as level as any slate-bed pool table, the white hare moving in odd looping angles toward the low bluffs across the river, a couple of miles away. The sky was that variety of high plains clarity found only upwind of cities, making me feel like the lone amoeba under a blue microscope.

Ben stomped on the accelerator, and the pickup jumped past me through the open gate, tires lifting October dust into my eyes and nose. I slipped the willow post under the wire loop and walked to the truck, Gillis standing on the wheelwell and licking my elbow as I went by. We bounced down the sandy two-track for a mile until it dipped into the first washout. Ben turned right, toward the river, paralleling the six-foot gully. Riley said he'd seen some sage grouse out on the flats that fall. On a warm morning like this, they'd be somewhere along one of the sage-lined gashes that cut across the flat. Ben looked more into the gully than ahead, and we made several trips over large stands of sage. A cow skeleton, still partially hung with Black Angus hide, showed up too late; the pickup lurched across ribs and spine and Ben's new twenty-gauge jumped out of the window-rack, falling behind the seat. He leaned on the brake, and my forehead bumped the dash.

"Damn, kid, whyn't you tell me that was there?" He took his pipe from the dashboard and put it in his mouth.

I looked out the window, not answering. The washout split up ahead. "See that line of sage? Why don't you drive along that and find a place to cross, and I'll walk down the crick toward the river. That way we can cover more country."

He shrugged, not looking at me, flicking the top of his lighter. I got out before he said anything, opening the tailgate for Gillis, unzipping the dusty case on the 97. I moved the slide back, then forward, then eased the hammer down and slid another shell into the magazine. Gillis whined as we walked past the pickup. I didn't look back, just heard the engine race and cow ribs crack as the truck jerked away.

I followed Gillis into the damp sand along the gully bottom. I knew damn well that at some point Ben would dump the pickup's front end into a washout or high-center another skeleton, and I'd have to drag out the shovel or jack. But for now I just wanted to walk here, along the bottom of the blue microscope. It was a pattern we repeated: the old Indian with the skin and look of a dour walrus and shiny new twenty-gauge, and the shiny new *wasichu* hunter with the Indian's rejected Model 97 Winchester. I needed him to show me the old trails, and he needed me to shout about skeletons and dig out pickups.

Gillis sniffed at white-haired coyote droppings, then trotted up out of the gully along a cow path. He knew it was time to be above the birds. As my head rose along the sage, I saw some sort of big raptor, probably a golden eagle, above the bluffs. The river flowed narrowly over there, taking a tiny slice of the plain, a reminder that a glacier melted along here before the Missouri changed course. Now the river did not fit the plains. I looked down at my smooth hands on the old wood of the shotgun, then turned and looked back at the pickup moving through the sage a half-mile away.

We found the sage birds another half-mile toward the river, the first a shadow that didn't fit the sagebrush. Gillis caught the scent in the last dew. The grouse started to run, black and white breast feathers coming out of shadow, then saw the dog, panicked, and spread its wings like a piece of sagebrush unfolding. The long barrel of the 97 moved up and then in front, grayed nicks barely catching sun, the bird a sort of Pleistocene megagrouse, too large for the now. It seemed to be flying toward the place where the river flowed larger, until the shot, the grouse turning slightly and dragging its belly over a sage top, dust rising around the sage as it fell beyond, one wingtip above the brush slowly easing and disappearing. Gillis ran, and another bird came out of the sage and fell, and then another. The last fell in the open, and I ran and picked it up: a hen. Gillis mouthed the big cockbird, trying to get a grip, then dragged it over, eyes over his shoulder toward where the third fell. I sat down and lay the two birds beside me, backfeathers the dull horizon hue of sage, the hen the size of a big pheasant and the cock twice as large. *Too easy, sometimes too easy to kill big things*, I thought, then picked up the cock and pushed a knife through the skin under the breastbone, suddenly smelling new blood like railroad ties in dusty heat, then reaching back into the heat to the throat and pulling everything out. The heart was almost as large as a plucked dove, and I put it back in the body. Gillis brought the other bird, a young male, then lay down and watched me clean the two smaller birds. I put them in my game vest, no room for the big one, and stood up. The pickup was down and wounded a quarter-mile away, the engine whining rhythmically. The big grouse balanced the weight of the 97 as we walked, Gillis hunting, flushing another jackrabbit, this one still half-gray. Ben had given up by the time we arrived. He sat in the open driver's door smoking his pipe, pickup angled down into a washed-out cowpath.

"Pickup sick, white man," he said, looking at the birds. "Good thing you shoot supper."

I lay the three birds in the truck's bed and picked up the shovel. "Good thing white man invent shovel."

Riley's ranch buildings lay in a scatter of white and red across the mouth of a big coulee at the edge of the badlands. I was still sweating from the shoveling as we drove through the gate, bouncing over the dried green evidence of many Angus. Riley was already out of the door of the white house, near white himself: hair and shirt and socks and pale washed-out Levi's. The ranch dog, a one-eyed blue heeler, ran up and shouted at Gillis, who shouted back.

"You look like you could use a cold beer," Riley said. Ben shook his head. He'd almost shot a friend during a whiskeyed-up poker game and hadn't had a drop since. Riley knew this, but asked anyway.

"I'll have one if you will," I said. We walked into the hothouse livingroom, warmed by the light of the picture window. We sat down and I looked at an old copy of *Western Horseman* while Riley got the beers.

"Found those sage hens," Ben said when Riley sat down. I took a long drink of Olympia.

"Didja?" He took a drink. "How many?"

"Three. The kid got 'em."

Riley nodded, looking at me, then back at Ben. We knew enough to say hello, even though I'd been there every week or two all fall, since hunting started. But Ben had known Riley's father, and since the wife and boys had left, we'd hunted the ranch more than anyplace else. Riley said, "There's some sharptails up the coulee toward the butte. Saw 'em yesterday. Good-sized bunch."

Ben nodded. "He might be able to hit 'em."

This was the way the conversation went, an odd triangle of three-quarters of a century, the youngest silent, the middle offering, the old pronouncing, mostly about birds, deer, cows, and wheat. A photo of Riley's boys sat on the color TV, two high-school kids in broad Stetsons, not yet as red-faced as Riley. There was dust all over the TV, too, but you could see where another photo had been.

"Say, Ben, I got a horse I need some advice on." Riley walked to the front hall and pulled on a pair of brown cowboy boots, too cowshit-covered to tell the original color. "He's right outside."

We followed him back into the yard, the heeler following us, looking back to make sure Gillis stayed put. The horse was a medium-size Appaloosa gelding. We leaned on the corral rail and looked at him. He limped just slightly, almost too little to tell it was on the right front hoof.

"Got banged up a little. Some cows got into that forty-bushel wheat up on the bench just before we cut it, two-three weeks ago, and I'd been riding the bay for a couple of days. This sonofabitch bucked me off right here in the corral and kicked one of the rails and cut himself just above the fetlock. I treated it but he's still limpin'. Think he'll be okay?"

Ben watched the horse for a moment, then shrugged. "From where it is, nothin' to worry about. If it was behind, maybe, but not there on the side." He knocked the tobacco out of his pipe.

Riley knew this. He just wanted to keep us there longer than a beer. He knew horses. "What you think made him buck like that?"

Ben looked at the horse again. "Ride him much?"

Riley shook his head. "No, he's my oldest boy's." Then, as if he'd heard somebody else speak, he stood straight up and pushed away from the rail, turning his head and looking off toward the reddish coal-lined butte at the head of the coulee. Ben turned and looked at me, then at the horse. Riley walked off a few steps, his back toward us, shoulders rising slowly, then falling just as slowly. He stuck his hands in his pockets and turned his head, looking west, lips white, then looked down at the ground again and kicked a piece of dry manure.

"They sure as hell don't give a man much choice," he said.

Ben cleared his throat and flicked his lighter open, sucking on his pipe. "If you can't ride this horse much, I'd put a bit on him and then tie the reins to one of his hind feet. Let him buck against himself for a while."

Riley's shoulders moved up again, then down. "Yeah," he said, still looking up the coulee at some cows. "That just might do the trick."

When we drove the road along the rim a while later we could see where the cattle had run into the wheat. Riley hadn't cut the area they'd trampled, and it stood like a confused thicket above the level stubble. Ben said it sure looked like it might have gone forty bushels. I looked back down the hill toward the ranch yard, now a quarter-mile back and empty except for the dog lying next to the horse corral.

A big patch of buffalo-berry ran down the other side of the coulee, gray-green like the sage but with a purplish undertone from the berries. The road followed the field and then turned left along a side coulee, opposite the brush two hundred yards below. Ben stopped the pickup. "You want to try that?" he said.

I nodded. "Meet you up top, on that trail on the other side of the butte." I got Gillis and my shotgun from the back, then headed downhill through scattered yucca and rabbit-brush, crossing a white-rimmed alkali spring in the bottom and angling up above the brush on the far side, Gillis at heel. I wanted to be above the brush before sending him in, so the sharptails would flush and flatten out below me instead of flying around the curve of the hill. We stood there for a moment, breathing hard together. Then I motioned with my left hand into a deer tunnel beneath the gray thorns. "*Get* the birds."

He trotted forward, putting his nose out tentatively to make sure no lone thorn-branch blocked the tunnel, then disappeared into the shadows beneath the shoulder-high brush. I heard him patter over dead leaves and then a sudden rush, rising into the sound of the first bird coming up, branches moving before the bird climbed through, a feather drifting back down as the sharptail cluttered higher. The shotgun was already up and I thought again *too easy, too easy* as the bird dropped back with the feather between the leaves. Then more birds came up even farther below on the edge of the hillside's curve. I missed one and then knocked feathers from another as the rest of the covey went out unseen on the bottom, sunshine side of the thicket.

"Damn." They should have been in the shade, up here. Gillis crashed around in the shadows below, stopped, then rushed again and started toward me steadily until his head came out of the tunnel again, a bird in his mouth. I could feel its crop stuffed with wheat like a small bag of birdshot when he lay the grouse in my hand, the strange furry legs, like a ptarmigan's, dangling below. The grouse was smaller and subtly browner than the sage birds, as if it drew some color from wheat and red hills. I put it in my vest and then started uphill fast along the upper edge of brush, in case a few more hadn't flown with the main covey, Gillis running tongue-out beside me.

Beyond the other side of the buffalo-berries, I could see up the rest of the long coulee, barren except for bunchgrass and yucca. Two birds were just disappearing on set wings into the brush at the base of the coal butte, a half-mile uphill. We ran down the hillside and then walked more slowly up the coulee bottom, panting and sweating, finding old deer tracks, the sharptail bouncing warm against my back, then climbing the base of the butte toward the brush. One bird went out far ahead, probably an old one from the year before, *clututlutl* sounding faintly as it flapped and sailed, a tiny movement with a shadow against the coal-vein, disappearing around the butte's curve. Climbing higher, I suddenly rose above the benchland wheatfields on either side of the coulee, feet crunching on disintegrated coal, and could see the river plain below, stretching toward the bluffs, so distant their irregular line looked like bright tan clouds against the horizon. I stood there catching my breath, looking up the sides of the butte, knowing Ben was somewhere in the sandy mushroom knobs beyond, standing beside the pickup and waiting for the sound of shots and wild grouse to fly by. I could go either way, up above the brush alongside the butte, or underneath this time, hoping they'd fly across the low pass into the barren knobs and Ben's gun. The sky seemed something other than a microscope now, perhaps a larger lens curving out and beyond the hills and underneath the horizon. Another sharp-tail flew from the open hillside in the sunlight, far too far away, and I thought, before I walked down into the thorns, Gillis breathing beside me: At least they give some illusion of choice. At least they give you *that*.

8

The Ninety-Seven

The first time I saw the 97, I knew where it came from: that era around the turn of the century when men still just hunted and really did not question why. It was something they simply did. You can see it in the eyes of the men in an old photograph from Michigan's Upper Peninsula, standing next to a cross-pole bending with a dozen deer; in the oak-dark oils of a painting of a grouse, a dog, and a hunter; in the wagon covered with waterfowl from Chesapeake Bay. You can hear it in the rhythmic words of Roosevelt's Africa: "Had lunch today beside the carcass of a beast."

The 97 came from a closer, more western part of the era. I'd glimpsed that time and place in my grandmother's old photograph album, of the early years on the homestead in central Montana. There was Grandma B. in a white blouse, long black skirt, and Stetson, holding two sage grouse she'd shot from the sky with the little twenty-two pump in her hand. There was the grandfather I never knew with a pronghorn buck, his Savage 99 in the crook of his arm. There were friends forgotten and friends known, standing over the body of the last grizzly killed in the Judith Mountains, the mountains that overlooked the homestead. Everyone in the photographs is black and white, no shades of gray, looking steadily forward into the eye of the old Kodak, no questions in their faces. Men—and women—had guns, and they hunted. They hunted animals they ate; they hunted animals they felt threatened their new life in the wilderness; they hunted because they enjoyed hunting. It was a way of life, and they never felt compelled to defend it, because no one ever attacked it.

The 97 was almost totally without blueing, the steel the shade of a prairie September thunderstorm, the "Model 1897 Winchester" stamped into the rail behind the forearm losing its sharp edges. The wood was dark, worn by hands, dented by wagon seats and pickup doors, scratched by wild rosebushes and buffalo-berry. It had the same texture and color as the face and hands of the man who owned it, my wife's grandfather, a Sioux Indian from the Fort Peck Indian Reservation. I saw it for my first time on my first visit to the Reservation after being married, when Ben and I went hunting. We went hunting because that is what men did.

We hunted all day in the grassy hills and badlands. It was mid-afternoon when we came to a patch of chokecherry, the last cherries drying in the sun. "There's always 'chickens' here," Ben said, taking the 97 from the gun rack. "You know how to work this?" I thumbed back the hammer, then eased it down, feeling the light action of the trigger. I pulled the forearm back, then pushed it forward, moving a shell into the chamber, and eased the hammer down again.

"Yeah."

We put Ben's dog into the brush. For a moment we heard her pattering through the leaves underneath the chokecherries, and there was a time of stillness, just a moment under the prairie sky, before I heard the chatter of birds and the hard burst of wings. A sharptailed grouse flew from the brush to my right, and I brought the old shotgun to my shoulder, brought the hammer back under my thumb, everything moving easily and exactly, as if laid out in vectors and intersecting lines. I looked along the barrel as it floated toward the bird, sensing for an instant the enormity of the sky and the smallness of the grouse against it. Then the brass bead on the end of the barrel swept in front of the bird's flight, a gleaming flight in itself, and the 97 went off without my choosing it to and the bird left the sky, simply, with no after-moment of feathers floating. Then another bird came up, flying away from me, toward the hill sloping beyond the brush. There was a consciousness of the action working, the feel of steel sliding against itself, and the bead was on the bird and another shot sounded through the rush of more birds rising to my left. I saw the far bird dropping as I turned and then heard two shots, saw two more birds falling, and then silence. The last empty shell was already in the grass, the last full shell in the chamber. I looked at Ben.

"Wait," he said. The dog ran unseen in the brush below, and a single grouse rose, fighting the leaves with its wings, so far away. The shotgun moved again, locked into its movement, and then, even farther away, so far away I cannot believe it even now in my mind, the grouse fell, brown wings the color of the cured grass, its falling the curve of the hills. That was all.

Ben drew on his pipe. "Good shooting, kid." He pulled the pipe from his mouth, looked into the bowl, then knocked the burned tobacco out on his hard palm. "But you know, that's a trained gun."

He had only the one shotgun. He was from that era, that sepia-toned time, when a man only had one shotgun, one big-game rifle, and a twenty-two. Over the next three years, when I came to visit, I used it. He did not. I didn't bring any of my own shotguns. Perhaps I felt he'd be offended if I did, but perhaps more because I wanted to shoot the 97. He would just stand back and watch me shoot, or drive down to the end of a mile-long coulee to wait and pick me up with my load of sharptails.

After the third year, my wife and I moved to the Reservation. I was beginning to sense that the era I'd seen in old photographs was still at least partially alive there, in Ben and the hills he'd grown up in. For some reason I wanted to find it, to be part of it and understand that life. Perhaps it was

THE NINETY-SEVEN / 89

nostalgia for the memories of my grandmother's photo album, but the desire was there.

So we hunted. We hunted for days across the open hills, hunted sharptails in the berry-brushed coulees, hunted white-tails in the wooded draws, hunted mule deer in the badlands, hunted pheasants and ducks along the sloughs of the Missouri. I learned the pattern of sharptail life across the fall, from the rosebushes along the wheatfields in September, to the buffalo-berry thickets in October, to the shortgrass along the plateau edges in November. I learned where the whitetails liked to bed and how to push the pheasants to the river's edge and then wait there, listening, shotgun held lightly, until the birds could no longer stand the silence and burst up through the snow. I learned how to pluck sharptails quickly, as soon as they'd been shot, when the feathers were easy to pull from the delicate breast-skin, and how to slice steak and roasts from a buck's hindquarter. That is what I did. I hunted and took care of game and tried to recapture an era, because that's what men did.

It was a cold evening in late November when I went to Ben's house to see if he wanted to hunt ducks in the morning. He was in his chair, puffing on his pipe, watching a football game on television.

"We'll have to wait until nine or so," he said, after I'd asked him whether he wanted to jump-shoot some farm ponds we knew, "I've gotta go to the hardware store in the morning."

"What for?"

"I'm gonna trade off that old gun."

"Which one?" All three of his guns were old.

"Oh, that shotgun. I'm getting too old to haul that thing around anymore. It's too damned heavy."

I couldn't believe what I'd heard. "You mean the 97? You're going to trade the 97? For what?"

"There's a real nice little twenty-gauge down there. Real light."

I shook my head to myself. I couldn't comprehend it. He'd told me so many stories about the old gun, about killing sharptails after his hunting partners had missed, about outshooting the trap champion of North Dakota on a pheasant hunt. I thought for a moment. "How much did they offer for it?"

He told me.

"Oh, come on. It's worth more than that."

"Hell, it's just a beat-up old gun."

"You really mean to trade it?"

He nodded, his pipe moving up and down.

"Okay. All right. Tell you what—I'll pay you that much for it."

His eyebrows came together. "Why?"

"Because I want it."

He shrugged. "If that's what you want."

My wife couldn't understand my excitement when I brought the old gun home. In reality, I didn't consider it mine, but a piece of time on loan: something of value that eventually would have to be returned. I was sure that Ben would regret his decision, especially when I placed the 97 in the line of guns in my cabinet, its gray barrel and battered stock saying so much more than the sharp new lines of the other guns.

We lived three years on the Reservation, but eventually knew we couldn't stay there forever. Life was too restricted; there were other worlds that we wanted. And I also sensed that the era I'd wanted to capture had been pushed to its limits, that its last moment there, in that remote part of Montana, was just that: something almost gone, and that perhaps its most valid place was in my mind, rather than my life. We moved to a small city in the mountains of western Montana, and I put the photos of the old life on the Reservation in a shoebox and stored them in a closet. Photos of Ben and me next to the pickup, holding two limits of sharptailed grouse, of us next to two hanging bucks, our rifles angled across our chests, of Ben taking a Canada goose from my Lab along the Missouri. Photos very similar to those old photos of the Chesapeake or the life on the old homestead, except that these were colorful Kodachrome, rather than black-and-white.

We visited the reservation each fall, and I hunted sharptails with Ben—and that was the only time I used the 97. Its full choke and thirty-inch barrel were totally impractical for mountain grouse; yet that wasn't the only reason I didn't use it in the mountains. Something had changed; the old gun was almost retired except for the prairie hunt each fall.

And then even those hunts ended. My wife and I separated, a separation much like the separation we had made with the Reservation. We each wanted other worlds. I almost acted on my original feeling then, the feeling I'd had when I first bought the gun, and almost returned it to Ben. But then I sensed that would just be a plea for the past. Perhaps I'd use it on my own sharptail hunts, wherever they were, as part of the memory of him and an era.

Then one fall the 97 never left the cabinet. I never made it east of the mountains to hunt prairie birds. It wasn't until the middle of winter, just before a trip to the trap range with two friends, that my hand impulsively took it from beside the new Remington and slid it into a case.

When I walked to the firing line, next to four men wearing vests covered with the patches of competition, carrying new guns equipped with adjustable buttplates and high ribs, and I saw the mountains beyond the traphouse turning pink with evening, a strange feeling came over me. It was as if the old shotgun and I, as its carrier, did not belong there on that concrete pad, between men dressed in bright colors and tinted glasses.

That feeling still lingered on the edges of my mind as I slid a shell into the 97's chamber, but it eased slightly as I brought the gun to my shoulder. The clay soared out against the mountains, and I swung with it; at the shot and the sight of the clay still sailing, untouched, the feeling returned. There was something wrong. The gun did not feel exact, smooth, the way it had on that day when I'd stood above a chokecherry patch with an old man. In an odd way, it was the same feeling: of the shotgun being detached from me, with a sense of its own. But now the feeling was of unwillingness, as if I were forcing a saddle horse up the wrong trail.

The first five clays went untouched. I wasn't aware of the other men; their words and shots seemed something on the edge of a dream, something I had to move around but not consider. The ninth clay was barely chipped, the first hit, and I tried to concentrate, to find the rhythm of the swing. I broke two in a row, and then everything left again; only three more broke, at uncontrolled moments, during the rest of the round. As I pulled the last shell from the receiver and walked away from the line, not even looking at the score sheet, I vaguely heard a slight laugh and comment from one of the other shooters. Suddenly I was angry—not at him, not at any mockery of me or my shooting, because I felt so apart from that—but at his smugness, his ignorance of what I held in my hand. I wanted to turn and tell him, coldly, of what that gun had done, of a thousand sharptails above the pale October prairie, of a pheasant dropped far off across a frozen river, of an old man with a face the color of walnut and how men once lived. I turned and looked at him; he looked away and turned toward the other men. Quickly, with that turning, all the anger drained from me. I stood for a moment, looking at the mountains, then walked slowly to the clubhouse, knowing I would never shoot the 97 at anything but wild prairie birds again. What it was and where it came from were something almost gone, and it should not be used in any other way. It was time to put aside illusions and live with memories. They are always much more kind.

9

The Rio Grande Turkey

The sporting literature of today regards the wild turkey gobbler with somewhat the same reverence once reserved for whitetailed deer and brown trout, ascribing levels of cognition far beyond those of lesser beasts, or even the average sophomore English Lit major. Hence we get phrases like "wily ol' gobbler" and "boss-tom of the ridges" applied rather indiscriminately to any male turkey able to make it past his first spring hunt.

In actuality, while turkeys have a skull filled with gray tissues capable of low electrical impulses (biologically, much the same system as an English Lit major's), those tissues still reside in the skull of a bird. To put it colloquially, turkeys have "bird brains."

Some turkeys, of course, have been conditioned (in much the same way sophomores are) to be half-smart. Most of these "educated" birds live in the East and Southeast, where their education—being harassed by humans dressed like trees—is more-or-less unavoidable and constant. But across the West, where their contact with hunters becomes haphazard, most gobblers exhibit traits much like those described by the hunting author "D.C." in an 1880 edition of the magazine *Forest and Stream*: "The wild turkeys are plenty here, and I think most of those who have given their attention to the bird will agree with me, that they are the wildest and the tamest, the most cunning and wary, and the most stupid and foolish of all birds."

"Wild turkeys are plenty here" could describe some private ranch in Montana, California or, especially, Texas, since the population density on any would probably be higher than a hunter from Pennsylvania or Tennessee could ever imagine. I just read an account of an eastern hunter's first Texas turkey hunt. The limit was two gobblers; he killed his first in the first half-hour, the second the next day. The story in between was mostly a desperate attempt to persuade the reader that these were indeed wily ol' boss gobblers, that every turkey hunter's life would be enriched by matching bird brains with the subspecies at hand, the Rio Grande.

Rio Grandes were originally found almost entirely in Texas, scientifically known as *Meleagris gallopavo intermedia*, since they are intermediate between the dark eastern turkey and the white-rumped Merriam's of the Southwest. To anyone used to looking at eastern birds, the difference lies in paler buff tips on the tailfeathers. To anyone used to hunting eastern birds the difference is striking. My good friend Jim Conley of Orlando, Florida, has hunted turkeys and guided turkey hunters across North America, and specializes in hunts for the most antihuman turkey of all, the Osceola. He put it succinctly and straightforwardly, the way he puts everything. "Rio Grandes are the dumbest turkeys of all."

But even if they are dumb—or, perhaps more correctly, naïve—they adapt very well to country much like their native Texas, hot and semiarid, with enough brush for cover but also extensive open areas. Just as the Eastern turkey does best in oaks and the Merriam's in ponderosa pine, the Rio Grande likes brush country, which is why it has been planted in other areas across the western Sun Belt, and even farther north, where it's dry enough, like the interior of Washington and Oregon. The Rio Grande, for instance, is the primary subspecies established in the place most of us would least associate with things wild and naive: California.

I ventured there one spring, with rather mixed feelings, primarily for a wild boar of (mostly) genuine European ancestry, but secondarily to hunt a Rio Grande gobbler. My mixed feelings came from the fact that, though I love to hunt anything interesting and edible, most people do not venture from Montana to California for that purpose. It felt like leaving New York City to visit the art museums of, say, Poughkeepsie.

If indeed such exist.

We crossed the Sierra Nevada on one of the lesser highways, from scenic Carson City (as one friend describes it, "just a little bit of sin"). As our half-ton pickup, feeling very Brobdingnagian among the Lilliputian cars of weekending yuppies from Sacramento, emerged into the foothills, I remembered the thought of California I'd had on my first visit twenty years before: This must have been pretty nice country before they filled it up.

We emerged from the mountains at Jackson, and soon thereafter saw a Rio Grande hen standing under a lone white oak on a hillside, probably wondering if she should go back and sit on those damn eggs some more. This gave us hope.

We drove down through the central valley, eating lunch at a Mexican restaurant in Hollister, the place that was supposedly "invaded" by motorcycle gangs back in 1947, inspiring the early Brando flick, *The Wild One*. As we ate, I remembered again Jack O'Connor's belief that hunters should travel overland to their destination, thereby gaining an appreciation of distance, terrain, and culture not possible in air travel. After driving through miles of nut groves, then eating tostadas in Hollister, I found the notion basically sound.

We appreciated other cultural differences when we hit the freeway heading south, finding that while it didn't measure up to the Long Island Expressway on a Saturday afternoon, it still seemed more crowded than the stretch of highway between the Musselshell and Big Timber. Which is why we were surprised, when we obeyed the printed directions to the ranch and left the freeway near Paso Robles ("Pass of the Oaks") to find ourselves almost immediately in a land made of green hills and orange poppies, the little valleys between filled with small white oaks, tall digger pines, and low chamiso brush—and less traffic and humanity that you'd find on similar roads around Big Timber during the tourist season in July. The unlined asphalt forced all notions of freeway from our minds as it turned among the small valleys and soon, just as it would in any other country as pastoral, turned to gravel. Six does, looking like miniature Rocky Mountain mule deer, stood under the shade of an oak in the gravel, hopping the barbwire fence as we passed. Farther on, a pair of valley quail flushed from the road's shoulder.

A boar was the priority, so I had only the rifle along that evening as we took a short ride up the canyon above the ranch house with one of the guides. We did see some pigs, a mama and about six little ones, that ran into the brush like a package of very quick Oscar Mayer hot dogs, legs masked by the spring grass. As they disappeared we heard a turkey gobble farther up the road. Around the bend we found a Rio Grande gobbler and four hens, the puffed-up gobbler parading back and forth like a bronze-and-buff vacuum cleaner fifty yards from where the guide parked the truck. We watched for a while, and then my wife got out and pursued them with a telephoto lens. They eased into the brush in front of her almost as slowly as the shadows of the pines.

"We don't harvest a very high percentage of our turkeys," the guide said, leaning on the cab. "The season's short, and most people are interested in pigs." I didn't say so, but thought about the difference between the way the pigs disappeared and the reluctant stage exit of the turkeys, and nodded. It seemed it would be hard enough to take a big boar, with tusks like the curved ivory handles of a Moroccan dagger, and easy enough to shoot one of the gobblers.

As that Spanish boar hunter, old Ortega what's-his-name, said in a different way: In hunting nothing is certain. Two hours after sunrise the next morning, I'd killed the biggest boar they'd seen on the ranch in several months. The guide looked at me and said, "Are you lucky?"

Late that morning, as Eileen and I watched my boar being skinned in the screened-in butchering room at the ranch, we heard a hen call from the nearest ridge. We found my shotgun and mouth-call and hiked up there, circling into the timber to come down on the hen from above. She seemed to be calling from the end of the ridge, just inside the trees, and our plan was to move up and use her as a live decoy in case a gobbler came by. I called occasionally as we advanced, to keep her vocal and located, the shade of the small oaks feeling nice after the climb in warm California sunshine, and almost walked right up on her as she came up the hill to meet us. She spooked and flew across a little canyon to the thick pines on the north slope and I said something that didn't resemble turkey talk.

As we headed down the hill back to the ranch, however, a gobbler sounded off from the very top of the ridge where she'd flown. We turned around and headed up, spooking a dozen deer from the trails under the pines. Near the top, I called once, and the gobbler answered from the next curve of the main ridge, two hundred yards away. We climbed to the very top and sat below some oaks, catching our breath.

To our left the ridge curved in a big horseshoe, the far side where the gobbler called. I called again and he answered, then appeared for a moment as he strutted under the ridgetop oaks. A hen and then another started calling to his left. I called again and he gobbled, but the hens also called, sounding farther away.

"We've got to move up fast," I whispered. "Maybe we can get between him and those hens." Eileen nodded, and we took off at a half-trot around the horseshoe, flushing a pair of quail that flew low over the grass and then landed and ran, just their topknots visible above the green. We eased through the oaks along the open south slope and stopped to call. Another gobbler sounded off on the next ridge, farther down. We waited, heard a hen cluck somewhere in the vague distance, and then took three steps forward and saw a turkey head disappear over an open rise below us. We sat under an oak and called again, but nothing answered. Dumb Rio Grandes.

Soon it was almost one o'clock, when turkey hunting legally ended for the day, so we walked back down the shady north slope to the ranch. Our friends Tom and Walter were there with two jakes they'd killed an hour before. They had gone out with Walter's drilling, with twelve-gauge barrels over a thirty-ought-six barrel, ready for turkey or boar. Tom called occasionally and two young gobblers had come in just as they were about to quit for the morning, unexpectedly, catching the two hunters in the open. Walter killed one when the birds came within thirty yards; when they walked over to pick it up, Tom called again and the other jake came back. Walter handed him the drilling and they soon had another crafty Rio Grande gobbler in hand.

The next morning we were in the back of the pickup, heading up the canyon where we'd seen the turkeys the first evening, where Tom and Walter had killed their birds. Eileen and I wanted to hunt on our own, so Tom and Walter and the guide were up front, on their way to search for a young eating boar; we were to signal when we wanted to be left off in the dark. It was barely slate light and as we passed under some tall digger pines silhouetted against the slate we saw a dozen turkeys roosted up there. They hunched their wings slightly but said nothing, so we waited until we were a ways up the road before tapping lightly on the side of the pickup, our signal to be let off.

That is not the traditional way to roost turkeys; but, after all, we were in California. We eased back through the pines to the edge of a clearing seventy-five yards from the roost. I pushed my back into a notch in some chamiso, while Eileen lay on the ground behind me, under another bush. I clucked very softly, and two gobblers each double-gobbled in the almost-dark, like a pair of drunken singers attempting a round of "Three Blind Mice" and not getting the timing quite right. Off to our left, above one of the pale hills, the sky turned just slightly paler, as if someone had flipped the switch on a forty-watt bulb. The gobblers went silent, and I heard the sound of big wings flapping once and then hissing down out of the trees.

I do not know about you, but even more than a wild turkey gobbling at first light, down there in some hollow where you absolutely know you can call him, nothing makes the skin on the back of my head contract more than the sound of wings gliding off the roost. It is just like, and yet not-like, that first instant where you see a trout rise under a willow shadow and know, without a doubt, that you have the right fly on the leader but aren't quite sure you can make the cast—and know you'll only have one chance. Soon I heard another pair of wings sail down, and then two more. By now there was enough light that I could see the birds as they sailed, just the slightest color in the grass and pines. And then a slightly louder hiss came down, and I could see turkey legs under the one small chamiso in the clearing, fifty yards away, and a gobbler walked out from behind the bush in full strut, head arched back stiffly as if he were a football player wearing a red neck-brace, beard dangling toward the ground like a short necktie. And then another gobbler strutted out behind him, as the hens began pecking at the ground, ignoring such odd and absolute yearnings.

I clucked again but neither gobbler responded, instead just staring at the hens in front of them, and I realized this was yet another typical Western turkey hunt, with too many hens around to call in a lonely gobbler. So I talked to the hens, clucking softly, responding to the rhythms of their voices, rather querulous and self-satisfied, exclaiming that yes indeed, over here I'd found a delectable bunch of pine nuts. They pecked their way behind the low brush, angling toward us in an erratic but determined line. One of the gobblers came from behind the brush in eager spurts, as if his braced neck hurt and he could move only when desperate need overcame his pain. I looked at him and had that odd realization that comes whenever you call elk to a bow or turkeys to a shotgun: *He's in range, and I can shoot him.* He was still inflated as tight as a rubber raft. You are not supposed to shoot them that way, since they may suddenly gobble, extending their necks and making you miss. But when I whistled he didn't move, so I put the old pumpgun's bead on his wattles and pulled the trigger.

We walked the mile and a half back to the ranch with the turkey slung over my shoulder, feet tied to neck with a short piece of parachute cord, arriving just as the sun came over the hills, scattering quail and blacktailed jackrabbits from the dusty two-track as we walked. And I thought: Sometimes I like them naive, for the hunting life is not all "matching wits" with things we want to kill for their flesh, but an excuse to enter another country, some land we have never seen before, and never would without this particular search. Turkey gobblers, or indeed brown trout or whitetailed deer, do not always have to be wily, but just themselves. And unless we change that by feeding them, or breeding them so that they become an extension of our own unfortunate domesticity, they always are—which is something that can't always be said for our own species. It is nice to look at something closely, even if it is not always wary, but just itself.

10

Good Eats

Two decades ago, I lived for a couple of years in southeastern South Dakota, where they have built a palace of corn snd made the ringnecked pheasant a country deity. I moved there just before the corn harvest and pheasant season, and quickly found that while corn people are about equally divided between boiling and roasting ears, there exists an odd unanimity about cooking pheasants.

The first time I mentioned pheasants was in my carpool, as we drove between green fields that obliterated the horizon. "Pheasants?" asked a woman about my age, an aspiring poet who wore her hair in long red braids. "They're *so* good to eat. You know the best way? Cut 'em up like a chicken, then cook the pieces for an hour with a couple of cans of cream of mushroom soup!"

I come from a family that prepared game with complicated epicurean procedures (possibly because my father wasn't much of a hunter, so we didn't eat much wild meat), so to me this sounded a little like Julie Eisenhower's favorite recipe, the one where she cut a Twinkie in two and topped it with a scoop of ice cream.

A few weeks later, I was at a party given by some of my wife's professors at the University of South Dakota, the sort of affair where the graduate students put on their best Salvation Army ties and eat as many hors d'oeuvres and drink as much wine as they can, since their usual diet consists of cheap peanut butter and turpentine beer.

Our hostess approached while I had half a smoked salmon in my mouth, and asked several small-talky questions. My wife answered while I coughed. This woman was one of the professors' wives, a tall blonde with naturally frosted hair, slender in a blue velvet dress she'd obviously picked up at one of Sioux Falls's finer establishments. She spoke with teeth clenched and lips smiling, like a corn-country cheerleader who had gone to Vassar. The talk was dragging when my wife mentioned pheasant season.

"Pheasants!" the woman said. "Oh, they're simply dee-lish. The best way to cook them is with a can of cream of mushroom soup. Don't dilute the soup and cook at low heat, and the meat will simply melt off the bones. It's scrumptious!"

Of course, pheasant à la Campbell's is a step up from the stuff most bird hunters eat in the field. I am speaking here of the frightful nutritional habits of the average urban hunter, who for a few short weeks each autumn can barely consider where he left that box of sixes he bought last week, much less such insignificant details as vitamins, fiber, and cholesterol.

The worst case I remember is that of Tony, an ex-Chicagoan whose skinny body belied his fall diet. We took a trip up along Montana's Hiline one November, in search of pheasants and sage hens and geese, driving my pickup camper, which I had stocked with potatoes, rice, homemade sourdough bread, salad fixings, and a few packages from my freezer—elk steaks and sharptail grouse breasts.

Although Tony consumed his share of the food I'd brought, each time we stopped for gas he emerged from the quasi-supermarket that the modern gas station has become with a small sack. From this he'd periodically lift something—usually while we drove, but quite often while we walked the edges of a wheatfield. It would disappear in his mouth long before any identification was possible. On rare occasions, he'd say something like "Wanna snfmbr?" Once I nodded and got a single Milk Dud.

But the capacity of Tony's skinny stomach never really came to light until the trip was over. The day after our hunt, I went out to straighten up the pickup and camper and found a pile—actually a nest about the size of an osprey's—of boxes and wrappers under the passenger side of the seat. The accumulation of a five-day hunt included the packaging from at least two dozen Hostess Cupcakes, innumerable salted nuts, various Milky Ways, M&Ms, and Milk Duds, three dozen sugar-coated doughnuts, two pounds of jalapeño pork rinds, potato and corn chips beyond count, and one large oatmeal cookie, evidently his single attempt at eating something semi-healthy. Behind the seat were a couple of dozen empty pop cans, with no pattern except they all contained lots of sugar and caffeine. No wonder he shot so quickly—and missed so consistently.

Unlike convenience stores, there are other things to be gained in country cafes besides a few inches of beltline. Once my friend Kirby and I were after pheasants in the Powder River country, staying at a local $10-a-night hotel. (Only bird hunters travel to places obscure enough for really cheap hotels to exist, and only bird hunters rent rooms in such establishments. Anglers stay in "lodges" on lakes or rivers, and big-game hunters live in tents, both a step up from the typical bird-hunter hotel.) We got up the first morning and drove down to the one cafe in town, only to find we were twenty minutes early. As a rule, country cafes do not open unless there's somebody to open for, so we sat there for a half hour with the heater running until the morning cook/waitress showed up. She apologized for nothing at all, then fixed us toast and bad coffee while the griddle heated. While she was burning our sausage and eggs (frozen hash browns on the side) she suggested that we not ask to hunt at the first ranch west of town, since they were "real stuck up" and didn't even let locals hunt. Instead, we should take the first left past there and ask her brother, who would be in his shop fixing the front-end loader all morning. There were some good coulees just loaded with pheasants on his place, she told us, if we had a dog that would work cattails. We did, and there were. We would've eaten the food anyway, since all we had with us was a bag full of candy bars.

All of this doesn't mean that bird hunters won't eat good food, but they must fall into it while chasing birds. Steve is an example. Steve's as round as Tony is skinny, but he's also an avid pheasant hunter. One year he read an advertisement in the classifieds of a hunting magazine for "Real Dakota Pheasant Hunting, Room & Board Provided." A family farmer was renting out his college kid's room, and his wife provided "Genuine Home-Cooked Meals."

Steve is from St. Paul and likes to cook gourmet dinners with wild rice and even wilder pheasants, concocting strange and wonderful sauces and selecting just the right wine for the meal. While the pheasant hunting along the most rural edge of the cornbelt sounded super, Steve wasn't sure about the home cooking, guessing it might be along the lines of microwaved turkey and lukewarm canned peas. But that, he reasoned, is the price you pay for good pheasant hunting.

Steve called me a month after the season ended, and when I asked how the "Genuine Dakota Pheasant Hunt" went, he sighed at the memory.

"It was fantastic, just fantastic!"

"A lot of birds?"

"Well, we shot a few, but the farmer's kids had been home the weekend before. The roosters that were left were pretty wild."

"I thought you said it was fantastic."

"Oh, it was. That woman, Marge was her name, she cooked for us every morning and evening. I think she spent the whole afternoon cooking. It was unlike any cuisine I've ever had before. . . ."

"Let me guess. One night you had real fried chicken with mashed potatoes and milk gravy with no lumps."

"How'd you know?"

"And fresh creamed peas, or maybe creamed corn, and homemade biscuits, and a relish plate with two kinds of olives, fresh carrots and celery, mild pickled peppers, and sweet pickles."

"We had peas mixed with corn, but how . . . ?"

"And for dessert, there was homemade apple pie with a flasky crust dusted with sugar, and real ice cream, straight from a corn-fed cow?"

"Exactly! Except she had pecan pie, too. How'd you know?"

"I've eaten there myself, Steve, on various lucky occasions. Not there exactly, but someplace like it. Some nights it's roast beef or ham, but the rest of the menu stays pretty much the same."

"Yeah, oh yeah! But there was one dish I just couldn't get into. . . ."

"Let me guess. Was it Jell-O salad, with lots of multicolored marshmallows, mixed with artificial whipped cream?"

"You're amazing! Except it was multicolored Jell-O, too—red, green, and orange."

"I've been there too, Steve. Believe me."

Yes, bird hunters eat like they hunt, and bird hunting is taking whatever turns up, despite what some pheasant tacticians would have us believe. Unless you hunt only at high-priced resorts, where the hunting is as predictably excellent as the shooting, you take what comes. Most of my friends and I hunt haphazardly, not necessarily because we can't afford the pricey hunting, but because that's what appeals to us. Bird shooting is the modern equivalent of hunting and gathering. You take a shotgun and a dog and start hiking, seeing what happens. That's what we evolved into once we quit surviving on fruit and came down out of the trees: lost and hungry bipeds.

The one real bird hunter I've ever known who prepared even halfway for a hunt was an older man who liked to go on sage-grouse marathons, the ultimate in bird odysseys. He would fix a ham sandwich in the morning, then ease it into a heavy-duty Ziploc bag and place it carefully in his bird vest. Then we would take off across the sage and the sandwich would bounce around on his back with his canteen and the can of dog food for his German shorthair, and maybe a field-dressed sage hen or two. We'd stop for lunch below a windy ridge, and he'd take off his vest and drape it carefully over a silver sage. Then we'd sit down and he'd take out his lunch.

First, he'd open the can of dog food with his Swiss Army knife, pouring the contents onto a handy rock and letting the dog eat while he unwrapped his sandwich.

One of the last times we did this, he pulled the sandwich out and looked at it very closely through the plastic. Three hours between a canteen and a can of dog food had not done it any good. In fact, it looked as if had already been eaten.

"You know, John," he said. "I've got to figure out a better way to do this. The dog's food is starting to look better than mine."

I looked at the dog. He'd already finished his lunch and was eager for more. "Maybe somebody has invented the canned sandwich."

"If so, it was a bird hunter." He pried his sandwich away from the plastic and chewed a corner. "You know, I just found a real good way to cook old sage hens."

"What's that?" I said, taking a swallow of my peanut butter and jelly, itself very flat.

"You cut one up like a chicken, then put it in a pot with some cream of mushroom soup for an hour or so. You can slice it with a fork!"

To tell the truth, it ain't bad.

11

Jumping the High Plains

There are three kinds of Western waterfowl water: ponds, "cricks," and rivers. We jump the first two most frequently because they are more ideally suited, both spiritually and physically, to tromping around in a pair of hipboots or (just as often) Maine Hunting Shoes. But the first thing to remember is to never, ever put any decoys on either one. Not only would such a hopeful gesture be pretty hopeless, except on a pond directly under the air route between a stubblefield and the local "big lake" (usually a well-used irrigation reservoir devoid of any shoreline cover except three picnic tables and a few geriatric worm fishermen and their motorhomes), but would likely be ridiculed down at the local saloon ("Hear what that Barsness did now? Arnie saw him down by the railroad bridge, carryin' a sack. Looked like it was full of winter squash, Arnie said, and he thought what would that guy be doin' with a sack of squash? So he stopped his pickup by the bridge and watched. It was full of plastic ducks!") or shot.

It is something we've either heard about or actually experienced: the slow realization that the brown-clad person walking bent over along the bank is hunting our decoys. Or perhaps we first know something's up when he (or she, though I've never known a female to stalk decoys, which may be of interest to those developmental psychologists still concerned with the "real differences" between men and women) stands up and vociferously expresses dissatisfaction after realizing this bunch of ducks will never quack. Squeak, maybe, in the ecstasy of plastic rubbing together in a camo bag, but quack or fly, never.

Out here it often goes even farther. I would guess the willful (if ignorant) shooting of decoys was at one time common, judging from the attitudes of some of the old-timers I've hunted with. One was in his late seventies at the time, which meant he grew up at the tail end of market-hunting. I was around twenty, just beginning to unravel the mysteries of the sporting smoothbore, when he showed me the string of farm ponds over near the Dakota border. He parked the pickup a quarter-mile from the first dam, along the two-track road that edged the brushy coulee below. Three scrawny cottonwoods indicated the ridge of the dam, itself so overgrown with brush and grass that it almost appeared a natural part of the geologic landscape. The November clouds fed across the sky behind the three trees like a soft mass of distant waterfowl, and I shivered in the wind as I fed shells into the pumpgun.

"There's always a bunch of ducks on this one. Walk up behind them trees." I'd hunted with this man often enough to know that "always" meant once every ten times, but that odd chance was enough. I walked the dry winding crick, finding skunk tracks in the frozen sand, then skirted the big patch of dry cattails just below the dam, taking the quietest route up the sloping face. As I poked my head over the dam, the pond seemed too silent for ducks—but that was only because they were all looking my way over their yellow bills, like absent-minded professors startled in the midst of a calculus dream. Then they noticed the shotgun in my hands and rose straight up in a leaf-flutter of green heads, and I somehow had enough sense to to pick out three individual heads and shoot and shuck, and shoot and shuck, until three red empties lay on the cured grass beside me and three mallards lay on their backs in the water, orange legs stretching and then relaxing. I watched the other ducks fly away across a dull yellow stubble-field, and then heard the whine of the pickup's engine coming toward me. I turned and walked back down the dam and leaned toward the open driver's window to gloat for a moment before letting his retrieving mongrel, half black Lab and half schizophrenic, out of the box in back.

He took his pipe out of his mouth. "I heard three shots."

"Three greenheads," I said. "Pretty good, huh?"

He sucked on his pipe, looking out toward the dam. "Shit, kid, my brother Bud got thirty-six with two shells here one day. What'd ya do, wait for 'em to fly?"

Do not use decoys.

The ponds are a rather straightforward proposition, after you've found the hidden ones and figured out how to stalk them. In a land of few really different landmarks, you soon learn to perceive the subtle architectural changes between the last old homestead and this one. Perhaps one has a rusting Cockshutt hayrake out back, the defunct company name always good for a chortle among hunters who haven't had a good laugh since Bud backed the pickup over his own shotgun that time. The level of cultural sophistication is not often very high on the high plains. I once lived in a small town up near Saskatchewan whose only movie theater was a drive-in, usually running scratched versions of four-year-old ninja flicks. One day, however, the local paper (once a week except Christmas, when it came out twice to handle the ads) said a double feature would be playing, featuring *The Texas Chainsaw Massacre* and the recent Woody Allen hit, *Annie Hall*. Some friends and I agreed we could sit through some chainsaws in order to see an Allen movie. When I drove up to the window, the owner notified us that they'd only be showing one movie, since the other "wasn't any good" and they'd sent it back to the distributor. Guess which.

So we take our Art where we find it: in the way the horizon bends just slightly as it nears a mountain range ninety miles distant, the curve and colors as definite and yet unreal as any bucolic Van Gogh. As with any good painting, the longer you look the more the vista changes, as lenses of cold air move down the mountain, shifting color and shape. Or we can look closely at the iridescence of a mallard drake in our hand, like the bright-and-dark of one of the jungle Rousseaus. Or we fill the emptiness with words, either from some distant urban world, or our own, like Thoreau in some almost tree-less, waterless Walden, remembering the time we jumped the geese from Halverson's pond under the moon, each time telling it with more geese, and more moons, each reflecting off a new wave in the water until we cannot count that high.

Such things do not happen with quite the regularity of metropolitan art exhibits, but they happen almost often enough. That is what the farm ponds are, places you can count on each season, like the changing of titles up on a mar-quee. We drive between them, along the edges of high empty fields, watching the paintings change.

The cricks are something else, though, the hunting more tactical and less visual, more like reading a trout stream. The ponds you just walk up to and wait for what happens; the cricks you must plan and stalk. You find yourself thinking exactly that while fishing them during the summer, either for the trout that live in the streams that flow from the edges of the mountains, or the sauger and catfish in the silted waters. Casting a fly or bait or lure, you think that this would be a dandy place to ambush a few mallards, with the deer path through the willows on the far bank where you could send the

Labrador, and the open place in front of the cottonwood tree
where you'd stand after giving the hand signal, waiting for the
birds to fly by, low and fast.

Sometimes it even works that way. Part of the time it's
like fishing a dry fly to riseless water, just remembering where
ducks have been and standing in the right place before
sending the dog through the screening brush. And part of the
time you sneak up behind a high bank with binoculars, easing
your head through a notch in the rosebushes to look down a
stretch of bright stream for the green heads. And in between
bends in the river, there's the same strategies and imaginings
of travel: crossing the riffle by the treestand, then swinging
up and around the thick brush by the swamp to come up
below the beaver dam. By God, you are smart and sly.

I remember the best time it worked. It was Elmer
Keith's first autumn (like the Idaho gun writer, he is simply
"Keith" to his friends) and I took him up the brown-trout
stream, scaring two big fish from water barely deep enough to
cover their backs as they attempted to spawn. I marked the
place in my mind for the next day—or to avoid when duck
hunting. Perhaps there have been too many weird TV
preachers and rock stars lately, but playing voyeur to the sex
lives of salmonids does not provide the old thrill anymore.

We came to the big bend above the beaver pond, where
the deep water curves around a point below a high cutbank.
The ducks would be at the head of the deep water, the riffle

above providing aquatic vegetation to feed on and the deeper water just below good paddling. I stayed twenty yards back and gave Keith a hand signal toward where the ducks should be. He hit the wall like a linebacker and the ducks went up almost immediately, two drakes and a hen, just clearing the willow tops within range for one shot, which dropped the trailing drake. I heard more splashing, and then Keith came galumphing up with the dead drake, dropping it as he came through the willows. He did that sometimes when he was young, usually with big birds like mallards and pheasants and sage grouse. He got to where I could see him and he dropped it, saying, You come and carry this damn thing—I've had enough. I can still see his point.

Of course, there are other times, like the day when we were hunting both pheasants and ducks. Keith put up a cock-bird from some willows along a wide bend and when I shot, a hundred mallards that had been resting on the other side went up. Did I kill one? Did I kill the pheasant? What silly questions.

The rivers, of course, are the big challenge, primarily because on the high plains they are very wide and shallow, high enough in the spring that much shoreline vegetation gets washed away or silted under. Come fall, most cover along the shore is very far away from the water, say a short shotgun shot of dry sand and then another dozen yards of boot-sucking mud. The birds usually hang out near shore, but near is relative when the whole river is only a few hundred feet wide. They can see you coming across the dry sand or floating down the river in your canoe.

So you jump the islands by floating down from above, scanning carefully with binoculars to see if any mallards or Canadas are resting in the lee water down at the tail. Oddly enough, you can see birds best from a quarter-mile above the island, because the prairie rivers wind back and forth so gracefully in the sandy prairie loam. Then you paddle like hell to put the island between you and the birds, beach at the upper end, then sneak down through the mini-forest. A prairie-river island has a definite pattern of vegetation. At the head are mostly dead cottonwoods and driftwood, overlaying thin ground cover, since this is where high spring water batters the headland. A third of the way down, you walk under big, live trees near the shore, the interior of the island fading to a grassy savannah bordered by knee-high wild roses, both grass and roses crisscrossed by paths of pheasants and deer. Two-thirds of the way down, the big cottonwoods grow smaller and fewer, since this is where newer sand has been deposited and younger plants grow—mostly willows, often in stands as thick and limber as young bamboo. You follow the deer paths, sometimes bending over in the warm October sun. In the sweating pauses you take under the willow jungle, there's the smell of sweet-raw willow bark and the warm rot of grass on damp sand, and you hope you don't jump a whitetail or three and send them leaping down toward the mallards you can now hear, talking to each other softly on the gravel bar below the island.

The willows grow shorter, mixed with woody forbs, as you crawl farther, and the sand grows wetter. It's all crawl now, the pumpgun held in crossed arms as you walk on thighs and elbows. As you snake through the last bit of covers you see their heads and tails bobbing and rising in the bright brown water, just on the edge of range, and you remind yourself to shoot once—that is all, any more would be wasted or wounding—and then if you fail to jump up and run in those hot hipboots through the soft, sucking sand to the firm gravel, your duck will be half-a-mile down the Missouri before you make it back to the canoe.

All contingent, of course, on not flushing a rooster pheasant before you get down there where the ducks live.

It is still pretty wild down in the Missouri bottoms—at least as wild as any plains places are these days, actually even wilder than they were fifty years ago—because some of the big mammals that we wiped out while civilizing the country have been reestablished. Elk and bighorn sheep, for instance, and once in a while I find a dog track much larger than even a huge Labrador's. Some biologists will admit, privately, that there are a few wolves down there, in the darkest heart of the breaks. And the old homesteads too-hopeful people built far down in the eroded gumbo hills have started to fall. You can float a long ways before seeing another human, or even any fresh sign of one. I have paddled three days without even spotting a distant horseman, filling my social needs by jumping bull elk from the willows as I crawled after some piddly little ducks. Now *that*, a Pleistocene deer on four-foot stilts, antlers whipping the leaves from the longleaf willows as his massive rump plows away above your head like, you imagine, the rump of an elephant would in other jungles, *that* pumps the blood into those tiny arteries near the surface of your skin, and the breeze feels somewhat different than it did a few moments before.

One day we saw birds through the binoculars that were just silhouetted heads above the sunny curve of a riffle, the long rush of water foreshortened by the ten-powers, the river falling just enough in a half-mile to hide their bodies and create the illusion that they stood up to their necks in rushing water. We dragged the canoe up on the headland beach and then stalked through the big gray dead trees and the sunlit open savannah, the rosebushes scratching our hipboots as if we wore some sort of impervious dinosaur hide. A whitetail doe and two half-size fawns jumped there, but went toward the river, not downstream. We sweated through the wind-tossed willows, the sunlight through them falling in undulating diamond-shaped patterns on my friend's game vest, and then crawled the last hundred yards. I didn't hear any hens talking, and thought perhaps the deer had made them fly.

A large smooth driftwood log lay at an angle between us and the gravel bar, so we crawled to it, got on our knees with heads bent low behind the elk-sized trunk, then nodded three times and stood. Three dozen Canada geese stood so close I could see the river light in their eyes, and then they shouted and flew, almost loud enough to cover the sound of the shotguns. One hesitated and then, flapping hard on a broken wing, fell into the shallow water over the gravel bar. We could see its neck arch and then ease as it died, and then we were over the driftlog and running, the sand and mud holding us back harshly, as if we should have hesitated before killing something so big. I reached the bird first and, as I bent to grasp its neck, noticed the same undulating diamonds I had seen across my friend's back, but this time in the segmented water flowing over the gravel. As I lifted the warm neck and turned, the reflection flickered up my friend's wadered legs. I do not know who killed the goose, and really do not care.

12

Rocky Mountain Duck Places

Now, I have seen the bayous and ricefields around Stuttgart, Arkansas, and a November sunset over the upper Mississippi cornfields filled with ten thousand geese. But none of these ever seemed to be real *duck places* to me, because the duck places I grew up with have surroundings to distract the eye between instants of downreaching webbed feet, things like blue-treed mountains and distant, massive river terraces covered with antelope herds. My duck places are only vaguely surrounded by highways and scattered ranches; there are still lakes out here where you can watch the sun come up from a cold seat in a duck boat and maintain the illusion that it is still very wild.

And even if not quite so wild as it was in 1805, when Lewis and Clark traversed the Lousiana Purchase, it still gets as cold, even on those tame lakes, when the air falls down the Yellowstone Plateau and funnels into the narrow valleys below, or flattens the cheatgrass along the Rocky Mountain Front. One November we eased a johnboat through skim ice along the south-shore delta of a duck place on the Madison. Mallards and widgeon and geese came off the terraced wheat-fields with the wind at their backs, so fast they seemed black sounds somehow seen in the dawn. Two black retrievers shivered, then jumped from the boat when we reached the lee of the point. They ran up and down the shore as we hurried the decoys into the gray chop, whining as ducks passed overhead. My companion ran the boat up a channel behind us, while I arranged the shells and coffee and shotguns in the box blind, and orange light began to surround a domed mountain called Sphinx along the range to the east.

And then we began to shoot. It was one of those days when there were no contemplative pauses between down-reaching webbed feet because, like the Blackfoot Indian legend of the hole in the earth that spews forth buffalo, the plateau wind brought endless waterfowl in sixty-mile gusts. A flock of canvasbacks came in so fast that my companion led the first one ten feet and dropped the third, the bird falling so far from the blind that the bigger Lab had to dive face-first through surf to make the retrieve. We shot and shot, missing ducks going out over the lake by not leading enough, then missing them again coming back as they held nearly still above us in the headwinds, our shot blown out over the lake.

In the afternoon the flat glassy light dimmed as a bank of clouds moved with grayed opacity over the Tobacco Root Mountains to the west. We allowed another half-hour, and that's when the geese came in, low over the water, silhouetted by the light refracted through the whitecaps. They rose above us along the shore and we each dropped one from the edge of the flock. I began gathering decoys in waves that rocked me from crotch to chest, while my friend went for the boat anchored in the black marsh behind us. He found the fourteen-foot boat flipped end-for-end by the gusts, upside down in the channel, the engine flooded with water and a headless decoy bobbing toward the lake.

After righting the boat we made one brief, frozen attempt to start the outboard. With a wet horizontal wind blowing, we walked the boat along a half-mile of shoreline, cursing creatively as we stumbled through weed beds or drowned driftwood. The dogs hunkered snow-plastered in the bow like black-and-white vultures. Of course no one else was fool enough to be out there; even the elk hunters were inside someplace warm. But that is one of the advantages of Rocky Mountain duck places. We may not have quite as many ducks as Arkansas or Iowa, but we don't have quite so many hunters, either.

The prairie and tundra of western Canada grow many of the birds that fly over the Rockies each fall, the great flocks dividing somewhere in Alberta, some heading down the Central Flyway and some the Pacific. Snow geese come down in tens of thousands in a funnel along the Rocky Mountain Front, a sudden movement of white sky stopped occasionally by reservoirs. Most head south, over the mountains and across the headwaters of the Snake toward Utah, Arizona, and Mexico, but a few turn southwest. I once stood on a ridgetop along the Idaho border in early November, fresh elk tracks in a foot of snow in front of me, and heard a high hoarse fluting, just barely audible over the sound of melting snow falling from lodgepole pines. Looking up, I saw a flock of snow geese moving slowly against a pale blue sky, perhaps a thousand feet above the ridge, holding themselves above the remnants of the trail the Nez Perce used to cross the Rockies to hunt the buffalo plains. I wished them luck; they would need it in California.

The prairie and tundra birds that cross the Continental Divide, leaving the Missouri and Platte, find ponds and river pressed between thick-timbered mountains. The glacial pot-holes and ranch ponds form strange havens, surrounded alternately by subdivisions and sagebrush, the sloughs along the big rivers bounded by mobile homes and ranchettes. These provide the most civilized duck hunting. Civilized can mean many things, one being waterfowl refuges where hunting space is allotted by lottery, or through standing in long lines in the predawn hours.

It can also mean comfort. I have a cousin who once lived next to a slough of the Bitterroot, the banks bordered by tall cottonwoods that almost blocked the Sapphire Mountains beyond. Her husband was an artist, duck hunter, and car-penter who was so astounded by this surfeit of water that he constructed an elaborate roofed blind down the slough from the house, with an old overstuffed couch, padded shotgun rests, ammunition boxes and a space for a small wood stove, the smoke vented behind the blind into bankside alders. We'd get up before dawn on November mornings and brew a fresh pot of coffee on the wood stove and shoot through the first rush of early birds, taking mallards and occasionally Canada geese as they followed the river's margins south toward the Nez Perce Pass. An hour later, my cousin would bring down a covered tray full of scrambled eggs, fresh trout, and home-made toast and huckleberry jam. I don't know how much the dawn preparation of those breakfasts had to do with their later divorce, but it may have also had something to do with the flooding of the slough each spring, often over the banks and into the house. He would simply pull on hip boots and go about business as usual, even cooking on the electric stove while standing in six inches of water, or painting his geo-metric acrylics while the flooding slough carried away their firewood. But the main point is that I eventually had to replace that duck place with something else.

The something else was not so luxurious, though still civilized. The glacial kettleholes of another valley, lying amid scattered wildfowl refuges, become very personal duck places when you toss eight or ten decoys across one on a warm morning in early October, and blue- and green-winged teal glide fast above the fakery in the darkness. From this perspec-tive, on the edge of a valley below the vertical face of moun-tains much like the Tetons, you can barely perceive the pastoral lines of the land, the county roads, square stubble-fields, and tall willow windbreaks of farms. It does seem much more civilized than the windy mini-oceans of the Front, and yet there's an edge here, provided by grizzly bears that come down into the valley from the mountains each year, eating sheep from those pastoral fields, scaring children waiting in line for the morning school bus, and once beating up a pheasant hunter who decided to try the thick cover along a creek, less than a mile from this particular pond.

There's no huckleberry jam in this brush-blind, just an open-choked side-by-side, perfect for the teal, gadwall, pintail, or mallard that come to the close decoy spread as the sun rises, lonely on this warm dawn. From a mile down the road drifts the distant popping of shots from hunters crowded around a refuge. It seems odd for a goose to be so important this morning, when this private world seems so perfect. By ten the birds quit flying, and the handful of teal and sackful of decoys feel heavier than any goose as I walk back across the kettled pastureland to the pickup. On the way back home there's a stop for a slow breakfast at a highway café, with time to wonder about big things, like grizzly bears and Canada geese.

The most far-gone goose hunter I ever met was the father of a rancher I once cowboyed for along the Yellowstone River. Eli Sr. was successful enough at raising Angus-Hereford crosses that he spent many of his later autumns trying to figure out how to get close to the geese that fed along the Yellowstone. The bottoms there resemble Nebraska more than Montana, except for the Charley Russell bluffs behind the river. The geese fly from the river to feed on the grain and alfalfa left after late summer harvests. Most hunters spread decoys around pit blinds or the brush along field margins, but Eli? Eli built a horse.

He sat up on the bluffs with binoculars and noticed that the geese gliding into his fields didn't shy at the cattle and horses grazing on the leftovers. It's illegal, of course, to use livestock to "harass" or otherwise get close to waterfowl, so Eli made a limbless horse out of half-inch plywood, with rope handles for the hunters at places appropriate for horse legs. And it worked.

Of course, there were minor diffculties, like the time his partner (the tail, since Eli as inventor always took control of the head) got his glove stuck in the rope. When they went to fling the horse down to shoot, the butt end stayed up in the air, jumping and flapping around and emitting unhorselike language. Eli got his shotgun up but couldn't manage to hit a goose. "It's hard to shoot," he noted, "when you're busting a gut laughing." Sometimes, too, they would be slowly "grazing" their way toward a feeding flock when one of the neighbors would drive by on the county road and stop to gawk at the fools with the toy horse. Geese did not hold for this, but between mishaps Eli got a few honkers.

He loved them, in the air or on the table, but most of all he loved their voices. In hot September we would drive down to the river in the early dawn, ostensibly to check the cows. We'd rock from side to side in the cab of the twenty-year-old Ford pickup (old rich ranchers don't get to be old rich ranchers by buying pickups every damn decade), headlights touching the big trees as we drove along the rough trail through the cottonwoods. He'd stop in a clearing somewhere and we'd step out, the first leaves of autumn under our feet, and listen. Soon we'd hear geese talking, usually somewhere distant, but sometimes the sound would come close and low, and as they passed we'd look up to see a black vee across the Milky Way and hear not just the sound of goose music but the rush of their wings, just above the trees. And then we'd go look for cows. That was a quarter of a century ago and Eli died closer to then than now, but it's still a pleasant fantasy to imagine the horse still leaning, rain-gray and splintered, against one of the barns, listening to geese just down from Alberta heading for the Yellowstone.

13

*How Not To Learn
To Hunt Ducks*

I was sitting listlessly in the living room one rainy September afternoon in 1983, outwaiting the autumnal equinox. A loaded, accurate water pistol rested in my hand, but the cat was bored with pass-shooting practice. My wife was off at the Salvation Army buying her fall wardrobe, so the only sentient being left to water-torture was my Labrador, but the look in his eyes kept my finger from the trigger. For a moment I considered turning the squirt gun to my temple, but restrained myself, remembering I was inside to keep dry.

In short, I was bored and blue. The reason? At the tender age of thirty, I'd suddenly realized I didn't know how to hunt ducks.

Ignorance of waterfowling craft may seem minor to some. After all, many male baby-boomers reached thirty oppressed by larger concerns, such as the inability to transfer youthful pinball skills to video games. But my duck affliction went deeper, attacking the heart of my chosen profession: that of outdoor writer.

In those days, outdoor writers were supposed to be skilled in all the main blood sports, rather than specializing in tuna winching, mouse arousal, or bourbon drinking, as so many do today. To admit that I didn't know how to rig decoys in a west wind or blow a highball was tantamount to confessing membership in Friends of Animals.

Not that I hadn't shot ducks in my life. Over the years I'd killed, plucked, and eaten about every variety of waterfowl west of the Mississippi, from teal to Canada goose, with a few coot and snipe thrown in. Indeed, the very first official game I killed in my life ("official" being any animal whose life is taken after the purchase of a hunting license and a long wait until opening day) was a mallard. But the circumstances surrounding the moment were my downfall.

That first official opening day began on the shores of a shallow reservoir in southwestern Montana, the sun still behind the mountains and widgeon whistling by in the dark. I was thirteen, freezing in winter clothes that had shrunk mysteriously in the sleeves and legs since the past winter. Four dozen decoys were spread in front of me, and I was sitting in a reed-covered duckboat, the familiar heirloom twelve-gauge double in my hands. This ancient fowling piece had apparently gained a pound each year of its life. No matter; I was out there, on the edge of a *real duck marsh* with a box full of *real duck loads*, and there were *real ducks* flying overhead.

As shooting light neared, I kept glancing across the lake toward the far shore, where the man who had put me in this real place had gone in his johnboat to pick up some goose decoys and his dogs. Shivering, I watched the lake turn orange. The man who'd dropped me off (Lord, I didn't want to shoot a duck until he returned, to make that decision by myself . . .) was a student of my father's at Montana State University, a trout fisherman and duck hunter from New York who masqueraded as an English major in order to live in the mountains. He was old, perhaps twenty-five, and wise in the ways of waterfowl. I don't think my father actually committed grade bribery to get him to take me out—their relationship was much closer than that—but it was a perfect arrangement. My father instructed him in the use of adjectives and transitions, while he taught a hunting-mad adolescent about reed blinds and hip boots.

The mallards came out of the sunrise, black under the line of mountains, so quickly that I couldn't consider options. The shotgun came up ponderously (at five-eight and a hundred-ten I could almost hide behind its barrels) and all that weight kept it swinging until the muzzles passed the lead duck. The shot boomed off across the marsh, coming back in faint circles like the wavelets on the lake. The duck wavered and fell, wings loose and uncontrolled, splashing down near the shore. I squirmed from under the reed-covered boards and stood, shaking, as I broke the shotgun and replaced the empty shell. Then I walked purposefully to the mallard—a hen—and pulled it from the cold water. As I felt it in my hands—cold-feathered and yet warm underneath, a drop of pink water-blood running down my thumb and into my sleeve—the dawn edged a little farther toward day and geese rose from the lake and flew in a long line against the haze of the blue mountains. Their voices were close, as if they'd just flown around a street corner, and yet they were too far away.

My tutor soon returned and looked at my duck and shook my hand. We sat in the blind and waited for more birds. He talked to them as they flew, telling them what a clean, well-lighted decoy spread we ran. They'd turn and listen and some would head our way and he would smile a small smile, as if he'd learned the secret of the Mona Lisa. (Ever since I haven't been able to look at a magazine print of the painting without imagining Mona in tule-reed camo with a hand-carved duck call around her neck.) He smiled even more as the ducks sideslipped into the decoys, just before we rose to shoot. Finally, toward morning's end, one bunch circled endlessly, squawking doubtfully at his call, until he insulted their ancestors in duck talk and they flew south in a huff. We picked up the decoys and went home.

That was the beginning. Over the years, he and I hunted the marsh together almost every season. He acquired fancy new duckboats, more and lighter decoys, better shotguns, and a few gray hairs in his beard. I acquired better shotguns and a few more pounds, and that was all. I freeloaded off him because his duck mania was insatiable, a hot desire that pulled me into its backwash for a long and windy ride.

I always helped toss out the decoys, but wherever he said. I sometimes asked why he put the pintails down here and the geese over there, but the answer always disappeared in the marsh-muck of my mind. I listened to him quacking and chuckling and honking and whistling at the birds, but caught only a few words of the conversation, as if dimly recalling a phrase of high-school Spanish. I used him and killed—not hunted—every kind of waterfowl.

That was the sudden realization I confronted on a rainy day in September. For seventeen years I'd been using someone else's knowledge and artful desire. It was hard, but in the end there was only one honorable course. I drove the pickup downtown and bought a duck call. I quacked on it that evening, to the delight of my dog and the bemusement of my wife, as I hauled out some old cork decoys my friend had given me years ago. The afternoon was spent reading *Misty Mornings and Moonless Nights* and memorizing how to set decoys in different winds. The decoys didn't need fresh paint, I decided, since it was early in the season and plumage would be dull, but they did need new anchor lines. I almost called my friend to give him a sample of my lowball, but decided no, I was going to do this myself.

Opening day found me and the Lab wandering among a dozen glacial potholes an hour north of town, potholes I'd jump-shot in seasons past. We walked around in the dark for twenty minutes, me loaded down under a bag of heavy decoys, the dog loaded with eight months of not mouthing a bird. When I found the pond I wanted the wind was almost nonexistent, but I placed the decoys carefully anyway, spreading them out to allow for the nice weather. Then we sat in the reeds along the shore, the dog shivering under my left hand, the call in my right. At legal light, six mallards flew over and I quacked at them. It must have been duck-cussing; they headed west and never looked back. Soon another flock came over. I remained silent and killed a drake.

The birds kept flying over our pond, and I kept trying to talk to them. A few appeared affronted but most merely avoided us, as if our decoys suffered from some contagious plague of the larynx.

After an hour or so I began listening to the real ducks around me, hearing their voices and what they said. I experimented quietly in the blind, in conversation with myself. *Quack?* I said. *Quack quack?* The inner mallard was emerging. *QUAAACK QUAck Quack. . . .* I was only talking to myself, but six birds came in. Startled, I quacked carelessly, and they left.

It was getting on toward noon, the sun slightly too warm on my light camo. The dog fell asleep. Finally I decided the ducks had quit for good and stood, stretching in the sunlight. Two ducks appeared in the east, flying high. Grabbing the call with one hand and the shotgun with the other, I said *QUACK*

QUACK QUACK QUACK QUACK! My dog woke up, nose in the air, and the ducks turned in instantly, like a flock of Labradors responding to a whistle. For a moment I thought I'd scared them off, but the dog saw them and picked up his ears. They were coming in. Bending low, I softly whispered *quackaquackaquacka* as if speaking in a marshy library. They set their wings while still above the rolling glacial shoreline, then tilted their tailfeathers down and settled in over the decoys, the sun hard off the oil on their wingfeathers, and I smiled.

14

Payment in Partridge

To me, if not to him, it was a serious assignment. The man who had put me in my first duck blind and told me to sit still, goddamit, who'd explained over and over to a skinny thirteen-year-old that you have to point the shotgun in front of crossing pheasants—this person was going to come and hunt with me on the plains of northeastern Montana. I'd been bragging about all the fine Hungarian partridge hunting we had, and now he was going to show up with shotgun and dog, expecting to see some birds.

There were birds around, but guarantee them? Usually we'd run across a covey by accident while out looking for serious game: sharptailed grouse or whitetailed deer. The partridge we shot were incidental. The only place I knew where Huns hung out was around the scattered abandoned farms that stand like huge gravestones above the cattle pastures and wheatfields, reminders of when families lived on each half-mile of prairie.

The buildings still standing are boarded up now, used as grain bins for the larger farms that ate up the old homesteads. When the snow deepens in the stubblefields, the birds live around the old farmyards, picking waste grain, hiding in the tall grass around the buildings and rusting grain drills and dead threshing machines. But snow wouldn't fall until November, at the earliest—a month away.

Then I remembered the Clothesline Covey, so named because we always found it around the edges of the Andresen farmyard. Occasionally we'd see them as we turned off the county road early in the morning, onto the farm track that led into the big sharptail coulees up Elk Creek; more often we found them picking grit late in the day, when we were headed home. We'd drive up to the farmhouse, knock on the door, and ask old Barney if we could hunt his Huns. He'd say sure, as long as we didn't shoot up his overalls out on the clothes-line. We'd always give him a bird or two, if they held long enough.

I somehow doubted Norm would want to walk the perimeters of a farmyard. But while thinking about the Clothesline Covey, I realized I knew where other coveys lived. The Cattle Corner Covey lived around a fence-corner between a cattle pasture and some wheatfields, where the grass grew high enough to hide. And Ericson's Covey, on hot days found in the spring-fed hollow that held the old Ericson farmhouse, but in cooler weather down in the dry creekbot-toms below.

Even then, when I realized that the coveys lived in certain areas, I remembered the times we'd hunted there and never found them. I would guarantee all the sharptails Norm wanted, and in some of those places we'd kill a pheasant, especially with two Labs working the thicker stuff. But he was interested in Huns, and I began to wish I'd kept my mouth shut.

It was mid-October when he and Sil showed up, late in the afternoon, with not enough time left in the day to really hunt. But our wives insisted we get the dogs out of the way while they fixed a salad, so we drove out to my "range" (a rancher friend's cow pasture) on the edge of town and patterned Norm's new goose gun, letting the two male Labs work off their standard territorial arguments. Then we went home and barbecued a few pronghorn steaks, watching the last sun leave the yellow-leaved cottonwoods along the river below the house. The sky was clear and huge, so much bigger than farther west where the mountains compress its borders. We could see the badlands south of the river, each blue shadow of the hills precisely visible through ten miles of prairie air. Even the two dogs, my Gillis and Norm's aging Chief, seemed uninclined to pursue their usual arguments.

The night brought one of those complete reversals that make the October plains so unpredictable. Dull metallic clouds moved low over the dun badlands, and the yellow leaves along the river blew down from the cottonwoods. Cured grass that the day before had reflected enough sun to make us squint was beaten flat by the wind. The temperature was near fifty, but the wind and low sky made us feel cold and vulnerable. We drank coffee in the warm house until mid-morning.

Finally the accumulated caffeine forced action, and we loaded guns and dogs and headed north to Ericson's. The place is a deep coulee on the side of a high hill, scoured out by a spring that even in late August gives up a few gallons a day. Approaching from the south, we could see only the tops of the tall cottonwoods that grow around the spring in the steep bottom.

On the edge of the hollow is the old house where Ericson and his wife homesteaded before World War One. They built the house, planted crabapple and plum in the spring hollow, and raised a barn up on the level hilltop above. Two years later Ericson died and his wife abandoned the place. The barn is now scattered over a half-acre of ground, sheltering only deer mice. The concrete foundation of the house, built into the hillside, is rotting with frost-action. Down in the hollow, the old well has collapsed. The only things untouched by nature's unconcerned hand are the half-dozen rows of Russian olives above the house, planted as windbreaks, and a few of the plum and apple trees by the spring. Occasionally Huns and sharptails can be found in the windbreak, and through September mourning doves flutter in and out of the cottonwoods. A few times I've jumped a white-tail there, and once a cow elk from the herds along the

Missouri Breaks— perhaps, like Chief Joseph, trying to make a run for Canada.

We parked above the windbreak and crossed the three-wire fence. I was hoping the Huns would be there, but usually by October they've scattered into the grassy draws that splay like veins below the spring. The dogs trotted between the Russian olives, and I heard the clutter of a sharptail. Norm headed quickly into the windbreak, shotgun across his chest, while Sil and I stayed on the near side.

Norm walked down the runway between the trees, Chief edging in and out of the crested wheatgrass between the boles, sniffing. A grouse flew, clucking wildly, in front of Chief; I could barely see its shape through the branches. Norm's shotgun came up smoothly and he shot quickly, but the grouse kept flying. It was still flying strongly when it left the trees, far out ahead of us, and I could see it set its wings and start to sail before it dropped over the horizon.

"Well, hell!" I said.

Norm looked at me. "That was a little far for improved-cylinder." I'd watched him change barrels at the house but thought he was changing to modified, my choice for Huns. I started to speak, to tell him that Huns weren't quail, that they were just like sharptails except smaller. And then I remembered all the times he'd coached a skinny kid on working aspens for ruffed grouse, and stayed silent.

There weren't any more sharptails in the windbreak, so we walked down to the homestead to let the dogs drink at the

spring. Norm was relaxed, looking over the house with a car-
penter's eye, but I still thought about the missed grouse. I
analyzed my intensity as we walked through the old house,
looking up through the wind-opened roof, through the parallel ribs of the joists, at the low gray sky. Perhaps I just
wanted to prove that I'd learned my lessons well. All morning
I'd been pointing out little things about the prairie, showing
him who I had turned out to be.

We walked outside and up the slope toward the truck,
the wind trickling down our collars. Maybe, I thought, I
wanted to repay some kind of debt, give something back for
what I'd received. A certain deflating knowledge went
through me, though, that there is no returning the time spent
with a young kid, no matter what he learns, about hunting or
the rest of living.

We got back in the truck and drove a two-track through
the grass, down the slope of a coulee into a half-mile-wide
creek bottom. The dry watercourse bisected two fields, one
fallow and the other wheat-stubbled. Tall patches of
chokecherry, serviceberry, and buffalo-berry grew along the
deep bends. We drove toward the tallest brush, very slowly,
the pickup rocking over the barren field. We were still two
hundred yards away when the Huns flushed, perhaps a dozen
of them, slanting slightly in flight, their brick tails not visible
under the distance and dull sky. They flew fast over the
stubble a quarter-mile to a patch of stunted ash and willows—

the knee-high forest that prairie people call "buckbrush," wherever it's found—on the gentle hill beyond the field.

"Wild, aren't they?" Norm said.

There was no way to approach them from where we were. They'd see us and fly over the hill, and beyond the hill was a wider creekbottom where we might lose them. I drove along the winding creek for a half-mile, found a place shallow enough to cross, then drove across the stubblefield to a shallow draw leading up the hill. We parked and loaded the shotguns and heeled the dogs and started up toward the top of the ridge. I still wasn't sure we'd be able to get close to the birds. They were very wild and in low brush, but maybe we'd be able to follow their flight again.

We walked the half-mile along the ridgetop, into the hard wind, and the covey flushed at seventy-five yards. They sailed back down to the creek, wings wind-tilting, into the brush where we'd first flushed them. "They should hold now," I said. "They're tired and the brush is thick. Go ahead and take the dogs down. I'll wait up here in case they come this way."

Norm looked at me. "You're not going to shoot?"

I shook my head. "These are yours."

He shrugged, and he and Sil called Chief and Gillis. I sat on the wind-flattened grass and watched them walk toward the dry creek, the curving watercourse still slightly green between the yellow and tan fields. The wind whistled flutelike in the muzzles of my shotgun; as they neared the brush I felt my fingers tighten on the stock. The two tiny humans walked deliberately along the creek, the black dogs weaving along the edge of the brush just ahead of the hunters. At that distance, everything seemed to move too slowly.

I saw their guns go quickly to their shoulders and a flock of tiny birds in the air, at first scattered and then swarming together like insects. I saw one bird fall in the brush and two in the field, and then heard the small popping of shots in the wind.

Norm had two birds in his hand as I walked up, Chief still hunting the other in the tall brush, Sil behind him. Norm handed them to me, one a bird of the year and the other older, all delicate gray and rufous brown. "A double," he said. "Chief's after Sil's. She got one, too."

"I saw them fall." I held the bird as Chief pushed his thick chest through the brush toward Sil, another small bird in his huge mouth.

"First double I ever had on Huns. You don't see too many where we live." He watched Sil take the bird from Chief's mouth.

"That's great," I said. "Really great." As I looked at the small birds, I realized that I could never repay my debts, because they never had existed. You can only repay things that are borrowed, not those that are given.

15

The Late Birds

We all know that the most pleasant time to pursue upland birds comes during September and early October, and that's when most of us out here in The Land of Large Hats go after grouse—always mentioning rattlesnakes, thick alder leaves, cactus, drought, and other hardships to our Midwestern friends who often can't legally hunt until the ides of October. Yes, indeed, it sure is tough hiking around in all that red and orange vegetation, under that seventy-degree sun, while the ruffed grouse hang out in indolent gangs along the cool streams and the sharptails come up in straggling rises perfectly timed to the breaking and reloading of a side-by-side. It is *hard*.

But the Western upland hunting that really separates the September dilettantes from those one friend calls "cowboys in the know" arrives later, when most native hunters are after wild animals that grow large antlers or honk or quack. I go after those things then, too, as that's the time to chase them—but am always thinking of an article angling writer A. J.

McClane once wrote about (of all things) bluegill fishing. In the piece McClane suggested that perhaps one ultimate point of sporting pursuit lies in getting to know a particular species throughout the year. This suggestion follows me into my own hard pursuit of wild birds past the ides of October, into the steeled edge of December days in prairie ridges. This masochism encourages the peculiar conceit that such over-bearing interest purchases the right of possession. Take my elk—please, take my elk—but the late birds are *mine*.

We tend to think of sage grouse as inhabitants of vast waterless stretches of sagebrush and alkali, and they do live there, in the parched Great Basin and other pieces of the Great American Desert. But the high sage valleys of south-western Montana and eastern Idaho are another kind of country entirely, surrounded by mountains that begin to turn white in early September, watered by beaver-ponded brook trout streams that in turn are bordered by some of the most fertile hay meadows in the West. Between the hay and mountains live the sagebrush and the sage birds.

The sage-grouse season ends sooner in these valleys than on the high plains, sometime in late October, but winter does come early here and the hard edge can be found even then. Parts of the upper Big Hole Valley, tucked into the shadows of the Continental Divide, only average a week of frost-free nights year. So it didn't surprise us one Columbus Day to have eight inches of snow fall in the high basin where Lewis and Clark met Sacajawea's long-lost brother and his band of Shoshones. We hiked the foothills in the blind light of a new sun on new snow, the pediplain stippled with sage, and a mile away the narrow meander where one of the Corps of Discovery "bestrode the heretofore deemed endless Missouri." A whitetailed jackrabbit bounded out from beneath one sage plant, near white himself, just a few gray hairs in his winter coat. To our left and beyond in the upper valley the mountains stood in the magnifying clarity of air suddenly stripped of all moisture by cold.

We found the first birds at the mouth of one of the side valleys. The black Labrador put up one at close range, the big grouse flying low over the white sage. At the shot it tumbled, and three more got up beyond. At the second and third shots more grouse rose far out of range, in fours and fives and dozens. As we walked through the powder, hundreds of birds rose and flew and settled again in the stippled white, as if each piece of sagebrush had decided to transform itself into a like-sized grouse and briefly fly, just to warm up a bit. Three or four hundred sage grouse wandered across the mouth of that side valley, driven from their summer homes by the deepening snow and cold, forced down like the mule deer and elk from the Tobacco Root Mountains to the east, a warm-blooded aquifer flowing between the sage. The birds hanging on our backs were chunks of ice we'd chipped off the edge of a river.

Something of the same can happen with the sharptails of the prairies. They begin to gather in November, especially if sudden cold comes down from Alaska and Hudson's Bay. There are no mountain valleys to descend from; instead, the birds gather around the windblown ridges where the grass seeds and frozen rose hips remain cleared by wind. Of course you could wait until a slightly warmer day, after the front has passed, but sometimes you *can't* because it's been too long in the cloistered house.

One late November day, my old Sioux grandfather-in-law and I went on a search for birds, finding a few last ducks on the unfrozen centers of farm ponds—but no sharptails at all, and it had been a good year. All the berry patches of September held big coveys. We drove to new places where I walked out the coulees and ridges, seeing nothing but a coyote that stood from the lee of a sunny slope and then moved out half-loping, a quarter-mile away.

The sharptails were in a similar spot, in barren knee-high rosebushes just below the crest of a ridge. I saw the first walking into the sparse border as my head came over the ridgeline, the bird just on the edge of range for the old double. I started toward the bird with the dog at heel; it rose, then dropped at the shot farther into the brush, and two hundred more rose in one collusion of wings, definitely not the straggling rise of early autumn. I shot again, and of course missed, numbed by the loud hum of four hundred wings. They flew and flew, over distant ridges toward Saskatchewan, fifty miles north, until they disappeared in the haze. They do not do *that* in September, either.

Ben told me when I returned with my lone bird that the best way to hunt sharptails in cold weather was to find where they roosted in the evening. When snow covers the ground they roost in trees, like a flock of small turkeys, to keep from being seen by coyotes and raptors against the white ground. The thing to do, he said, is to take a twenty-two and shoot the bottom one first, then the next to the bottom, and so on until you reach the top of the tree. If you shoot any of the others first, it falls through the birds under it and flushes the whole bunch. Of course I was a sporting *wasichu* hunter with my side-by-sides and desire to shoot birds flying, but in his description I could see the grouse in a spare cottonwood against the white land, and could feel the need to kill them right in a cold barren winter, to have them all tumble one by one from the branches, so that hungry humans could eat. That's what we saw that cold day on the ridges: the hard edge of survival in that hard northern land. Above the prairies live ruffed grouse and blue grouse, throughout the major cordilleras and also on the isolated "island" ranges that rise above the wheatfields and badlands like the blued apexes of gentle tipis. Geologists say these turned into islands during the last ice age, glaciers forming the ocean all around; before, they had been mere high places in the vast spruce forest that covered the north country, full of woodland creatures like caribou and timber grouse. When the ice receded the islands lost their caribou, but some of the trees and the grouse remained. The highest ridgetops are essentially tundra overlooking the Missouri Breaks, and once or twice I've hiked up there, beyond where blue grouse live, to permafrost caves where it would be no real surprise to find the bleached antlers of a big caribou bull, or the tusks of a mammoth.

In those serendipitous years when an elk or deer makes its way into the freezer early (and even if one doesn't) there's time to take the side-by-side after mountain birds. They react differently to the cold than do prairie grouse; early in the year you're likely to find both ruffs and blues in family groups, ruffs along the creekbeds and blues on the high crests of ridges, grassy on one side and conifered on the other. Later, they're more often alone, or perhaps in pairs. And because the leaves have fallen, both from aspen and ground brush, they tend to fly more than earlier in the season, instead of walking stiffly off like feathered diplomats.

The blues, it must be noted, move higher as fall progresses (or declines—take your choice), one of the few wild creatures with such a strange tendency, a response to their ground-feeding. The high ridges are swept clean by winds, while the lower slopes they preferred earlier lie under deep snow. This is the reason why many elk hunters find them, and why many bird hunters (who have more sense than to climb up there in early winter) do not.

One year, though, with a cow elk sliced and frozen by late October, I decided to try one of the ridges winding two thousand feet above the creek that flowed through the small city where I went to college. The climb was pleasant, the day just cool enough to keep from working up a sweat, but it was rather disconcerting to the elk hunter up on top, to meet someone with a bird vest and light twenty-gauge. He said he hadn't seen any birds, but had seen a few tracks. I said the same thing about elk, and just as we decided to go our separate ways a blue grouse essentially fell out of a young Douglas fir on the ridge's shoulder and sailed perhaps halfway down the mountain, paralleling the route I'd just climbed. This takes some spring out of the legs.

But ruffed grouse are different. For one thing, they live lower down, where the snow doesn't stay until late November. After the leaves have fallen in October and grouse move out of the creekbottoms and onto the lower ridges— where fields meet aspens and aspens border conifers—they can even give the illusion of Eastern shooting. Every year there seem to be more of us who emulate the New England pa'tridge hunting ideal: the side-by-side, the thorn-tattered shooting vest, the ham sandwich shared with the loyal dog at midday, followed by a contemplative pipe as the hunter leans his back against an old stone fence and wistfully fans the tail of the single King of the Gamebirds he's managed to scratch down during the morning. My favorite grousing spot, a tributary off one of Montana's famed trout streams, even has a semblance of a stone fence. Well, it isn't actually a fence, just a big stone fireplace built in a Forest Service campground by the Civilian Conservation Corps back in the 1930s. But it's big enough to be *part* of a fence, and will have to do, since most fences out here consist of three or four strands of barbed wire and aren't too comfortable to lean against.

About every third time I've hunted this place I've glimpsed a fellow traveler in the pa'tridge world, an older guy who, whenever he sees me, eases quietly up some side draw with his Brittany, perhaps because I don't follow the ideal completely, despite my side-by-side and tattered vest. In front patters one of those damn Labs, a breed considered a near must by many traditional Westerners, due to the eclectic nature of our bird chasing. But my Lab, I suspect, makes me suspect to this wraithlike brother of the alders. Or perhaps, just perhaps, he's a transplanted New Englander, classically closemouthed and standoffish, waiting to see whether I really am one of the faithful before politely breaking open his shotgun, clearing his throat, and introducing himself while I'm sitting on my stone fireplace eating a sandwich. I've never gotten close enough to see if he wears a tie while grousing, as I've heard real pa'tridge hunters often do. On the return from such trips, I am tempted to talk of having "moved" such-and-such a number of birds, and to lay a hardwood log on the fire, if we had any decent hardwood around here.

The late shooting, when I get out there, is even more enjoyable than earlier on. The leaves have fallen from the deciduous trees, and since the foothill ridges are usually made of a mixture of open conifers hemmed by aspen down toward the river, the shooting becomes easier, even if the birds are more scattered. Something about this time of year makes me think this is what New England grousing is all about, that fertile fallen leaf aroma in the air, the world all tans and grays, the grouse very much the same color, and the sound of their hard wings muted by fallen leaves. The birds seem to fit their landscape more gently as they fly at obtuse angles through the barren trees, low solstice light sifting diffidently through the branches, and it seems we should speak quietly here. During the week I'm not even likely to meet any deer hunters on the grouse ridges, because they've pushed "farther back," and the world is left to grouse and fools like me.

I've hunted these birds not just with Labs but with various Brittanys, but one of the best was a Boykin spaniel that belonged to a friend. One day we were easing down a long flat ridgetop in late November, just where the big Doug firs meet a huge stand of aspens, when the first bird whirred off low and almost straightaway. As the gun reached my shoulder, the second bird took off from the right in a looping angle behind the first. When the first dropped to the open barrel I moved the muzzles up and left and shot as the second grouse flew behind a very sparse aspen top. Branches fell and a few dry leaves sprayed, and we heard a soft *whump* on the hill beyond—which turned out to be a large branch and not the legendary double bird, though the Boykin tried hard to find two grouse to retrieve. He died later that fall, and his owner a few autumns later, in that same canyon— perhaps the purest form of hunter's luck.

Farther down, below the ridges and foothills, the rivers flow mostly to the Gulf. Here the landscape is most changed: by fields and county roads, broad white-frame houses and railroad tracks, and by those two foreign birds, the Hun and the pheasant. You'll find both in other places, of course, but you'll never find more partridge (out here we pronounce the first "r" in the word—if we bother to use it) or pheasants than along the edges of bottomland fields.

I have never seen a bird more addicted to "structure" than a late-season Hungarian partridge. Early on they may be found anywhere in a mile-long stubblefield, but later they seem to adhere to stacks of haybales, fence corners, or an old homestead. Of course they evolved in eastern and northern Europe around the earlier grain-growing versions of most of our northern plains settlers—Slavs and Scandinavians and various Teutonic types—so surely they must have a particle of some chromosome dedicated to steppe agriculture. Finding a covey in the lee of an old homestead always makes me feel not exactly uneasy, but as if something else is going on here, some layer of time that runs counter to the ancient association between dogs and humans, perhaps that moment when hunters first scattered the seeds of wild grasses, dogs became more companions than hunting partners, and the wild birds of the steppes started living close to our leavings in winter.

But then a covey—or, rather, three coveys combined into one super-covey of forty birds—takes off from the downwind side of the old house, just out of twelve-gauge range, and flies down the coulee below the haystacks and over the rusting hayrake and old tractor to light in the crested wheatgrass along the stock dam. As we hurry down, they flush again just inside range, and I shoot one and watch again, while the dog runs after the dead bird, as the covey soars down the coulee toward the homestead. We hurry again, trying to catch the birds before they can catch their breaths, and when we do we're in the middle of the thirty-nine, half coming up ahead and half behind, and still I manage to keep my head and kill one. The bird lying on the frozen bare earth seems made of homesteaders' colors: the browns and grays and reds of the soils that grow wheat and oats and barley.

The pheasants bunch, too, often in bachelor groups, the cockbirds gathering in the brush near the stubble. The opening-day hunters have long since gone, the young birds that were going to fall have fallen, and only *survivors* are left. One fall Kirby and I hunted the Musselshell, stopping at every farmhouse along the way. We found an older couple, living in one of those peeling white-frame houses, with a new kitten that ran up my arm and onto my shoulder when I bent down to scratch its ear. The woman said, "Oh yes, and if you get one could you bring back some of the tailfeathers?" She liked to arrange long feathers in vases with wheatstalks and pussywillows and cattails. We said we would indeed, and started down a line of bare orange willows along an old river channel. The temperature was somewhere near zero, the wind cutting through four layers of wool and canvas, the dog shivering and frost-whiskered as he quartered through the cover. Far over the ponderosa bluffs on the other side of the river, six geese flew against a sky too cold to be blue. I thought about the warm ranch house where one of Kirby's cousins would serve Thanksgiving dinner later that day, and guessed that Kirby thought the same.

When we found the pheasants, they were buried in the snow along the willow roots, seven cockbirds that came up twenty feet away, showering particles of bright ice. Too cold and too bundled, we both shot the same bird and as he fell in the stubble the others flew across the Musselshell to a big patch of buffalo-berry. We took the one bird from the dog, as brightly tactile against snow as September aspens and scrub oaks against a dark juniper mountain, and then walked to the river's edge. The shoreline had gathered thick ice, yet the channel showed patches of open water. We called it good and walked back to the farmhouse with our pheasant, plucking the longest feathers from his tail, as the dog ran ahead through snow as light and dry as cattail seeds, looking forward to being warm.